The Classical Seven Planets:

Source Texts and Meaning

by

Charles Obert

Foreword by

Nina Gryphon

Almuten Press

Published and printed in the United States of America

By Almuten Press

3507 Taylor Street NE, Minneapolis, MN 55418

ISBN-13: 978-0-9864187-5-4

https://studentofastrology.com

Dedication

To Master Astrologer,

Teacher

and Student in Astrology

William Lilly

Acknowledgments

I want to give special acknowledgments and thanks to my mentor and friend Ben Dykes, who vary graciously granted me permission to use the descriptions of the planets from his forthcoming translation of Abu Ma'shar.

Thanks to my friend and colleague Nina Gryphon for providing the Foreword, and for good discussions about astrology and philosophy that helped to lead to this book.

Thanks to the people who took the time to read and critique a pre-release version of this book, including Rebecca Bihr, Madeleine Youngstrom and Darleen Yuna.

Also by Charles Obert

Introduction to Traditional Natal Astrology: A Complete Working Guide for Modern Astrologers (2015)

Using Dignities In Astrology (2018)

The Cycle of the Year: Traditional Predictive Astrology (2018)

The Lots of Fortune and Spirit: An Exploratory Study (2019)

Saturn Through the Ages: Between Time and Eternity (2019)

All of these books are available at the usual retail outlets. There are also downloadable PDF ebooks available at the site, https://studentofastrology.com

Table of Contents

Foreword

One of the challenges facing students of traditional astrology is the absence of a sufficient number of hands with which to keep multiple books open for easy comparative reading. I am joking, of course, but with a grain of truth. Texts comprehensively collating ancient planetary associations have been scarce despite a growing number of traditional texts available to modern readers. Perhaps one reason has been the incredible pace of translations published by Dr. Benjamin Dykes in the last decade; simply assimilating the new (to us) material has been a full-time job for even experienced traditional astrologers. Yet, in addition to expanding our own understanding, we need to help the next generation of astrologers. Astrology students have needed a contemporary comparative text that combined the best of traditional sources, and ideally, provided a modern commentary on sometimes obscure astrological attributions.

Until Charlie Obert had asked me to review the manuscript for *The Classical Planets*, I had wondered why no one had yet written such a text. When I read the draft, I understood - selecting the right sources and providing thoughtful commentary takes insight and a substantial amount of work. Charlie's book is a model for the creation of comparative texts; one must approach the sources with humility, care, and humor. At times, ancient authors may not align, or may disagree outright, and it takes patience and insight to tease apart the sometimes tangled textual clues. I am happy to report that Charlie's book does all this masterfully.

Foreword

As a practitioner and teacher of traditional astrology, I know first-hand the importance of students' command of basic concepts. The associations of the seven visible planets may seem completely rudimentary, basics that the student should have mastered in the first few months of astrological study. However, all too often, students' eyes are first drawn to the more esoteric occupants of the chart before (sometimes) turning to the less exotic seven. *The Classical Planets* is a much-needed corrective that restores the classical planets to their rightful place and draws out the complex, multi-faceted meanings of each of the seven divine planets. In the classical tradition, the visible planets were the vehicles of the gods. The deeper our understanding of the planets, the better our astrology, and even more importantly, the closer our approach to the divine. Whether you are a student or teacher of astrology, I predict this book will become a much-needed companion on your journey toward the stars.

Nina Gryphon

May 2020

Introduction - the Purpose of this Book

Learning Traditional Astrology

I want to talk about why I am writing this book.

I have spent much of the last several years of my life teaching traditional astrology. This has been largely through formal classes at Kepler College. I have also been leading study groups, mostly consisting of people with a modern astrology background. Based on that experience I am writing this book to fill a need I perceive.

I am now convinced that if you really want to learn traditional astrology, it is very important to learn how to work with ONLY the classical seven planets - Moon, Mercury, Venus, Sun, Mars, Jupiter, Saturn.

At least for learning purposes this means leaving out the three modern outer planets, Uranus, Neptune and Pluto. It means leaving out the asteroids. It means leaving out any modern planetoids or dwarf planets. It means leaving out any hypothetical points like Uranian astrology's Trans-Neptunian Planets.

I want to make very clear that I am NOT saying that all of those modern factors are not valid or meaningful or that they do not work in practice. I do not mean this book to be an attack on modern astrology, so please do not take it as such.

As a teacher I have watched people with modern astrology backgrounds approach learning traditional astrology, and I am convinced that there are important features of traditional astrology you will miss if you do not learn how to limit your work to the seven classical planets.

The Modern Approach

I have quite a bit of experience watching modern astrologers, both how they read, and how they go about learning traditional astrology with a modern background. This is what I have observed.

First of all, many modern astrologers rely very heavily on the three outer planets, leaving the classical seven to be a kind of a secondary background. It is very often the case that, when I put up a chart to be studied, modern astrologers will tend to jump first to the three outer planets, and there seems to be a special fascination with Pluto.

I find that modern astrologers who use asteroids tend to jump right to the specific asteroids they are interested in and make those the primary focus of the reading. The asteroids become the meat of the interpretation, and the seven classical planets are either ignored or serve as a kind of neutral background.

For me this approach to astrology lacks a sense of relative importance and of proportion. Even for modern astrology I think the core meaning resides in the classical seven planets, and all of the other points are secondary, and provide supporting meaning.

Adding in an open-ended number of asteroids and minor planets presents an additional problem: selectively choosing only the asteroids that support the meaning you wish to draw from a chart. Taken to an extreme, given enough asteroids and minor aspects to choose from, you can make any chart say anything you want. While I doubt this is done deliberately very often, I think it is far more common than people realize.

In astrology there is already a very strong tendency to project one's own opinions and biases onto the symbols in the chart, and having an essentially unlimited number of points makes that far more likely. The tendency is to focus on the points that support your desired interpretation and to ignore the rest. It is the astrology equivalent of news reporting that takes sound bites out of context and makes them the focus of a story; the danger of bias and distortion is common and widespread. This has been particularly evident in astrology interpretation of political subjects that I have been seeing recently, which overwhelmingly follow the opinions and bias of the person doing the reading.

Dignity and Debility

It is important to use the system of dignities and debilities with the traditional planets to weigh the varying strengths and weaknesses of planets. (Note that the subject of dignity and debility is outside of the scope of this book. I will discuss resources to learn that in the closing chapter.) Weighing dignity and debility is the heart of traditional astrology technique. The modern outer planets and the modern bodies like asteroids have no dignity or debility, so there is really no way of weighing their quality or strength in the chart. If you are familiar with traditional astrology this is a large loss. Without the rules of dignity and debility the temptation with any planet is to give it whatever meaning, positive or negative, that best supports the point you want to make. The rules of weighing and deciding with dignity and debility go very far towards making interpretation more balanced and objective, and less dependent on subjective interpretation.

Keyword Approach is not Traditional

The approach to traditional source texts that I am presenting here is a very different way of learning from the modern approach of starting with summary keywords.

With the keyword method of learning planetary meanings the tendency is to boil each planet's meaning down to a single core concept, and make that the point of focus. Or, you might have a group of related keywords, and interpretation is taught as the art of combining keywords, sort of like making a keyword stew.

Introduction - the Purpose of this Book

This core concept approach is especially strong in systems like Uranian or Harmonic astrology, where an extreme complexity in the geometric part of the system necessitates simplifying the meanings of the planets. Extreme complexity in one area necessitates simplification in other areas. For example, in David Cochrane's Vibrational Astrology system he boils the meaning of the planet Saturn down to the concept of trimming away excess fat. Now that could be part of Saturn's meaning, but it is by no means all, nor is it one of the most important or central concepts in the traditional usage of Saturn. In fact, if you look through the traditional texts we present here, you will not find a phrase anything like that.

You will see the single core concept approach very commonly used in modern beginner's astrology texts. This simplified keyword approach, going from generals to particulars, is not how traditional astrology is organized, nor is it how it needs to be learned.

In the traditional source texts we will look at, the listed meanings of each of the planets are not consistent. They are not organized around a single concept or keyword. You will see that the descriptions of the planets are more like catalogs, descriptions of attributes, of the kinds of items that are under that planet's jurisdiction. Each planet does have its main themes and characteristics, but they are complex and varied. The organizing concepts and understanding need to come AFTER you have been wrestling with all that detail, and not before. The system starts with learning particular meanings and moves toward the general concepts, not the other way around. It is a different way of learning, and I think it produces a much richer end result.

In the traditional texts there is a lot of overlap in the meanings attributed to the various planets. There is no good way to neatly say that this planet means x and that planet means y.

We also need to recognize that the traditional meanings are contextual, as much of astrology was used to answer specific kinds of questions.

For instance, as parts of the attributions you will often see catalogs of different kinds of plants, food, places, animals, stones, weather, and so on. Which list you would look at would depend on the topic of the question being asked. There is no single, one-size-fits-all keyword that can be applied to all situations.

The way we are presenting the source texts here is to present the texts with their details first, and the commentary and summary at the end.

Change in the Planet Meanings

Along with a change in style of learning there has also been a change in the meanings of the planets in modern astrology. This means you may need to make an effort to set aside what you already know about the planets and be open to meanings outside of that range. You will also find that what you think of as main modern meanings do not apply.

For instance, traditionally the planet Venus has little to do with money or wealth or possessions; it is at most a minor theme. That is a modern innovation that comes from strongly identifying the meanings of planets and houses. Venus gets identified with the second house so it must have to do with money. In traditional astrology that does not apply. Money and commerce show up most often with Mercury, and wealth is best attributed to Jupiter.

There are many other instances where common modern meanings of the planets are not found in traditional astrology, and we will address those with each planet.

Loss of Complexity of Meaning

With the keyword approach the meanings of the traditional seven planets have become greatly thinned out and reduced, and are much more one-dimensional. That is one of the reasons that modern astrology relies so heavily on the outer planets, asteroids and other objects - they are needed to complement and flesh out the very limited modern meanings of the classical seven. When the fuller and more complex traditional meanings are recovered there is much less need to resort to extra objects to flesh out the meaning.

In order to learn the full richness of the traditional seven planets it helps greatly to learn to read by limiting yourself just to those traditional seven. If you do not learn that, the tendency is to leave the classical seven as a kind of a thin and bland neutral background, a vague starting point, and to make the really juicy details come from all the exotic outer planets, asteroids and so on.

Traditional Astrology not Primarily Psychological

Modern astrology for the most part leans heavily towards giving the planets a primarily psychological and internal meaning. Modern astrology starts by showing how each planet represents a part of the psyche, where Sun is you main identity, the Moon is your emotions, and so on. You will often see it phrased something like, this planet represents the part of you that does x.

Traditional astrology does not work that way. In traditional astrology the meanings of the planets are primarily external, objective, and measurable. There is a psychological dimension included, but it does not dominate. You will see each planet identified with different kinds of people, of buildings, of places, of plants, of herbs, of foods, of body types, of diseases, of weather, and so on. The majority of those meanings have little to do with being parts of the psyche.

For instance, the Sun in traditional astrology has little or nothing to do with identity, who you really are. In traditional astrology the subject is represented by the Ascendant, the ruler of the Ascendant, and any planets in the first house. The Sun has a whole different set of meanings aside from that, and it can sometimes be a very unimportant planet in the chart and have little to do with your identity.

My Own Experience

I want to talk a little bit about my own experience, my own history working with astrology. I started out many years ago - many, many years ago - many, many, many years ago... as a modern astrologer, largely because that was what was available when I was learning. When I began to get serious about learning traditional astrology, I went cold turkey and cut out all of the modern planets and asteroids altogether. For three or four years I restricted myself to only the traditional planets, and only traditional meanings and techniques. I immersed myself in traditional astrology on its own terms.

After that, I went through a period where I added the three modern planets back in, experimented with modern techniques like the use of the asteroids and with analysis methods like Uranian and harmonic astrology. It was a very good learning period, and it gave me a great deal of respect for what is good about modern astrology.

The first four books that I wrote prior to my recent book on Saturn all came from that period in which I used the modern planets. In those books I tried to use a combination of charts where some were limited to the traditional seven and some included the modern outer planets. I did this partly to provide a kind of bridge for modern astrologers to approach traditional astrology, and in that respect I think they serve a useful purpose.

Earlier in this essay I talked about the reasons why I decided to return to heavily emphasizing the classical seven planets. In my current astrology work I now use only the traditional seven planets. My plan is to continue using only the classic seven in any new books and classes I do. That is based on my experience both in reading and client sessions and in my teaching classes and leading study groups. I find there are some things about the traditional seven planets that modern astrologers just do not catch if they continue to use the modern planets.

Even during my period of using the modern outer planets, I could tell that I did not think about them in the same way most of my students seemed to. For me they were peripheral, secondary to the classical seven, and for a good portion of my students they were the most heavily emphasized, the first points in the chart to be looked at. It now seems best to me as a teacher to emphasize the importance of the classical seven planets by removing the outer planets altogether. The seven classical planets will return to center stage since they will be the only actors on the stage, and this forces you to look at them in a new way.

My own experience in reading charts both ways is that having in the modern extra points, even just the three modern outer planets, does not add more information and detail, but rather adds confusion and noise. I find reading with only the traditional seven planets to be clearer and cleaner. I have had experience both ways, with and without the modern outer planets, and I now greatly prefer reading without them.

The Learning Exercise

If you are a modern astrologer, consider my suggestion to read with only the classical seven planets as a learning strategy. I am convinced from experience that if you really wish to learn traditional astrology it is necessary to build on the traditional rich meanings of the classical planets. That can best be learned by limiting yourself to using only those traditional seven.

Again, I want to emphasize that I am not saying that there is no merit to modern astrology, or that the modern outer planets and the asteroids have no meaning. I offer this book, and the use of the classical seven planets, as a useful way to approach traditional astrology. I also think the experience will deepen and enrich your understanding of these main planets, and that they will take on further meaning. Once you have gotten a feel for traditional astrology on its own terms, you can then decide for yourself how to proceed with your further practice. Whether or not you decide to use the modern outer planets and other bodies, I think you will find that the classical seven planets will take on greatly increased importance and richness of meaning.

Planetary Meaning - General Context

Here I want to sketch out some of the main concepts that provide a context for the planets in traditional astrology. Note that most of this chapter is adapted from previous books of mine.

The Traditional Order of the Planets

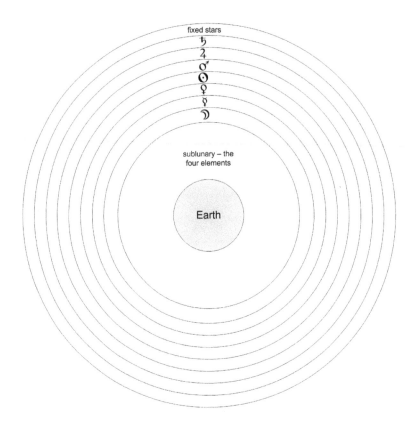

The worldview of traditional astrology is geocentric. The earth is at the center of the universe, and around it there is a big bowl, a vast closed dome, cavern or sphere, called the firmament in the opening chapter of Genesis in the Bible.

The outermost ring of this cavern is the Prime Mover, or Primum Mobile, source of all, eternal, and the realm of the highest deity. Just within that is a sphere of the fixed stars. They were called fixed because it was thought that they never changed their position in the dome relative to each other. Hence, they were fixed in position like lights attached to the dome.

Within the sphere of the fixed stars, there were spots in the sky that changed their position over time. These are the planets, from the Greek phrase *aster planetes*, meaning wandering star. Each of the seven classical planets, including the two Lights, the Sun and Moon, has their own sphere or orbit around the earth. The planets are like lesser gods or mediator beings that transmit the will of deity from the primum mobile down into our sphere of the earth. Each planet has its own domain of responsibility and its own way of acting. Each of the planets inhabits its own ring or heaven counting outward from the earth, with Saturn being the seventh heaven, the outermost before the realm of the fixed stars.

In the realm of the stars and planets all is eternal. The movement is orderly, regular and predictable.

The planet closest to the earth is our Moon. Within the Moon's orbit, is the sublunary sphere, the realm of change, of birth, growth, decay and death. This is the realm of the four ancient elements, fire, air, water and earth. The elements are in four rings inside the Moon's orbit, with fire outermost, then air, then water, and finally earth, the densest of the elements, at the center. It is the interaction and transformation of the elements that causes change on earth. The planets act on and affect the realm of the elements, and each planet has its own elemental affinity.

The Traditional Order of the Planets

The order of the planets in this diagram is the Chaldean Order. Starting with the Moon, the planets go in order of distance from the earth - Mercury, Venus, Sun, Mars, Jupiter, Saturn. This order plays into their meaning. As examples, some of the Saturn's meaning are derived from its being the furthest from the earth of the planets, right on the border between the moving orbits and the unmoving fixed stars.

The order of the planets also relates to the periods in human life - the Moon rules over birth and infancy, Mercury gets childhood, and so on out to Saturn which rules old age.

In the discussions of the planets, especially the general essay on Saturn, we will be talking about how much of astrology is built on paired sets of opposites. The prime set of opposites is Spirit and Matter, and in the Chaldean order, spirit is up at the top, outside of the fixed stars, and Matter is at the center with Earth. The seven planets are all mediators between the two ends of that set of polar opposites.

As you consider the meanings of the planets, keep this Chaldean order in the back of your head, as it will often shed further light on why planets have the attributions they do.

The Four Elements

When we talk about the world of the elements, we are in that realm called sublunary, within the orbit of the Moon. Outside of the ring of the Moon all is ordered and stable; within that order all is shifting instability and change, the mutable world of earth.

The four elements in astrology are made up of the 4 qualities, in two pairs - hot and cold, and moist and dry. We will first examine the qualities, then combine them to look at the elements.

Hot and cold are considered to be active qualities, moist and dry are considered passive.

Hot and Cold - Table of Qualities

Hot	Cold
moves up	moves down
expands	contracts
active	passive
moves forward	retreats
speeds up	slows down
advances	withdraws
adventurous, optimistic	cautious, pessimistic
diurnal	nocturnal

Hot and cold are the two opposite kinds of motions, like the rhythm of breathing out and breathing in. Hot is a motion that moves up, forward and outward, and cold retreats, pulls in, and retracts. It's like the difference between summer and winter - our bodies open and expand into the heat, and withdraw and contract to protect from the chill.

Moist and Dry - Table of Qualities

Moist	Dry
connects	separates
flexible	rigid
softens	hardens
receptive	unreceptive
blurs distinctions	accentuates distinctions

The Four Elements

Moist and dry are a different kind of pair. They are related to the movement of coming together and of separating. We talk of bare bones or dry facts when we want to look at things distinctly, to separate them. Adding moistness connects, but it also blurs. When things dry up they are lifeless; we need to add moisture to reconnect and form new life or sustain existing life.

Now take those two pairs, combine them in the 4 possible ways, and you get the 4 elements.

Elements by Quality

	Dry	**Moist**
Hot	fire	air
Cold	earth	water

Given those basic qualities, we will now examine the four elements in turn.

Fire - *hot and dry* - active, optimistic, moving, and ascending. A good element to get things done, or at least get things started. At the same time, the dry aspect of fire can make it rigid, not always flexible, drawing boundaries, making distinctions. Fire is considered diurnal.

Fire is active, but it needs but it needs air, and it needs earth, the most passive of elements, to feed on. Fire signs can provide energy, but they can also feed on, and burn up, the people around them.

Fire is light, so it is related to vision, seeing.

Fire is active but not reflective, not self-aware. Also, fire moves quickly.

Water - *cold and moist* - passive, receptive, cautious and descending. Water flows in all directions and takes the shape of whatever container it is in. It is a good element to slow down, pause, meditate, draw inward, and connect things, smooth off hard corners.

Planets in water are more sensitive, emotional, introspective, receptive, and internal. Water is considered nocturnal. Also, water is reflective.

Water flows downward as opposed to fire flowing upward. So, fire tends to be more optimistic, water tends to be more pessimistic or cautious.

Air - *hot and moist* - combines some of the activity of fire with the connectivity of water. Air also 'flows' but outward rather than downward, and tends to escape out of containers. Air connects by moving sideways, blowing where it will. Air is associated with intellect, communication, exchange of ideas. Air, being warm and active, is considered diurnal. Air is a social and mental element.

Earth - *cold and dry* - rigid, stable, passive, unyielding, but also supportive. Provides the shape, the container - without earth the other elements would have no way to keep a shape. When completely dry, earth is hard. It takes water to soften and loosen the earth, make it pliable. Too much water and earth loses its dry quality and its shape altogether, and it can be washed away. Earth is associated with material reality, practicality. Earth can also be sensual, in touch with the body. Earth also slows down any planets in it. Earth, being passive, is considered nocturnal.

These 4 qualities are looked at as pairs of opposites.

- Fire boils water, water extinguishes fire.

- Earth contains or blocks air, air flows around or disperses earth.

The elements are not stable and static conditions. They are continually mixing, blending, changing into each other. The four seasons are an image of the four elements set into cyclic motion, transforming one into the other. They seasons take the elements and combine them with the process of time.

The Elements and the Planets

The basic definitions of the planets are *partly* derived from their elemental structure. The elemental makeup of a planet helps to explain how it functions. The planet is not reducible just to its elemental quality, but that quality is an important part of the planet's identity. It says a lot about how that planet functions in the realm of the elements, what its affinities are.

There are some disagreements and inconsistencies in the attributions of the elements to the planets. The ones that I am using here go back to Ptolemy.

Planets by Element

Planet	Elemental Makeup
Sun	moderately hot and dry
Moon	very cold and moist
Mercury	varies by position
Venus	moderately cool and moist
Mars	very hot and dry
Jupiter	moderately warm and moist
Saturn	very cold and dry

The Sun is moderately hot and dry - it is life-giving, but can be harmful. When a planet gets too close to the Sun it is considered to be Combust or burnt up by the Sun, which is one of the most debilitating conditions a planet can be in.

The Moon is cold and moist, passive, receptive. It is considered to be the wettest planet.

Jupiter and Venus are both moderate, and both moist. Jupiter is moist and moderately hot, Venus is moist and usually described as cold, or rather, cool. Jupiter is moist in an expansive, outgoing way. Venus is moist in a cool, receptive way.

Some traditional sources show Jupiter as cool and moist, and Venus as warm and moist. Both are considered as moderate either way. I think it makes more sense to make Jupiter warm since it goes with the expansiveness, and Venus cool since it goes with a more passive receptiveness. Also, Jupiter is a warm day planet, and Venus is a cool night planet.

Mars and Saturn are both extremes - Mars is extreme hot and dry, Saturn is extreme cold and dry. Both are threatening because of their very imbalance and extremeness.

Mercury, again, is considered to be ambivalent. It is sometimes described as natively cool and dry. Some say it changes depending on whether it rises before or after the Sun.

Also - important - it is very common to say that Mercury takes on the characteristics of the planet(s) it most closely aspects - notice, not the sign it is in, but the planets it aspects, which is an example in traditional astrology of planets being more important than signs. Realistically, in my experience, the meaning of Mercury needs to take both sign and aspected planets into account.

Sect

Sect is built on the most basic two-fold division of astrology into day and night, diurnal and nocturnal. The planets are divided into two groups by sect along these lines, as shown in the following table and diagram.

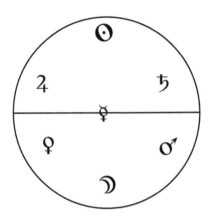

	Light	Benefic	Malefic
Diurnal	Sun	Jupiter	Saturn
Nocturnal	Moon	Venus	Mars

Each of the two sects contains three planets - one light, one benefic (beneficial and easy) and one malefic (harmful, challenging, difficult).

The sect of Mercury can vary, and it is determined by its position relative to the Sun. Mercury rising before the Sun is diurnal, rising after the Sun is nocturnal.

Sect is an overall chart dignity that sets planets as in or out of sect depending on whether or not they agree with the sect of the chart. Think of the division of sect as being like a pair of teams or political parties. It is primarily a political term and has to do with team membership and support. It also connotes family or tribe, being an insider of a group and having group support.

Thema Mundi and Rulerships

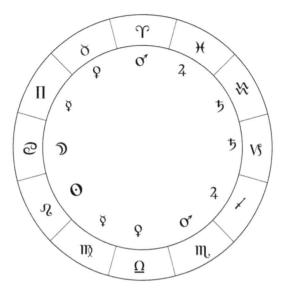

The Latin phrase Thema Mundi means world chart. It is a teaching device showing the signs and planets at the mythical creation of the world. The sign Cancer is rising at the left side of the diagram, and the traditional planets are shown in order based on their relative speed and distance from the earth.

The Thema Mundi diagram shows rulerships. Sun and Moon, the two lights, are on the left side of the diagram in Leo and Cancer. Cancer to Aquarius is the Lunar half of the circle, Leo to Capricorn is the Solar half. The other planets each have two signs, moving out from the lights in the order of their distance from the earth. Mercury takes the two signs adjacent to the lights, Gemini and Virgo, and so on out through to Saturn which takes the signs opposite the lights.

Exaltation

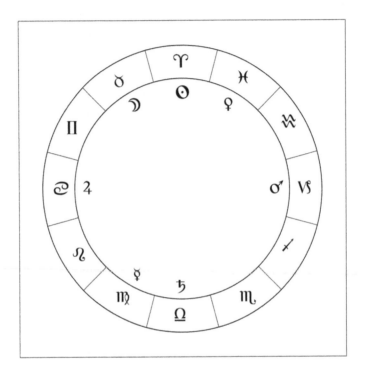

The diagram above shows the signs in which each planet has the dignity of exaltation. It is likely that this was derived from a separate rulership scheme than the rulerships we see in the Thema Mundi shown previously.

In looking at the two diagrams showing rulership and exaltation, it is worth noting that the planets pair up in opposition to each other in different ways. For instance, Jupiter is opposite Mercury in terms of rulership, but opposite Mars in terms of exaltation. It is well worth meditating on the two diagrams and considering how the different pairing reflects on their meaning.

The Joys of the Planets

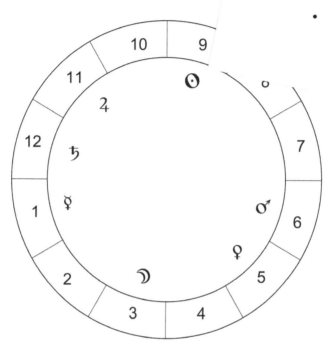

The diagram above shows the houses in which each of the planets is in their joy. In considering this diagram, note the following patterns.

- The two lights, the two benefics and the two benefics are opposite each other.

- The benefics are in houses considered fortunate and the malefics are in houses considered unfortunate.

- Considering the two malefics, Saturn or Mars being in its joy does not mean it will be favorable, but that it will be strong. Saturn is described as having its joy in the twelfth house because it delights in causing malice.

- All of the diurnal planets are in houses above the horizon, and all of the nocturnal planets are in houses below the horizon.

we have seen before, the exception to these pairings is Mercury. Mercury sits in the first house, right on the boundary line between the top and bottom of the chart.

The Source Texts

The historical information here is from ***Biographical Dictionary of Western Astrologers*** by James Herschel Holden, M.A.

The astrologers range from Vettius Valens in the second century A.D. up through William Ramesey and William Lilly in England in the 1600's, near the end of what is considered the age of traditional astrology. What is noteworthy is the consistency of meaning throughout that period spanning around 1500 years. This consistency of meaning gradually fell apart after that period with the decline of traditional astrology, and the meanings changed drastically in our modern era from the early 20th century and beyond.

Vettius Valens (120 A.D. - c. 175), born in Antioch in Syria, was a Greek astrologer and a Roman citizen. His textbook on astrology, named ***The Anthology***, is the earliest reasonably complete working textbook from a practicing astrologer that we have from that period, and it includes more than a hundred example horoscopes. His work has been receiving wide attention since its translation into English by Robert Zoller of Project Hindsight, and there is a public domain English translation by Mark Riley that is easily available on Internet.

Abu Ma'shar, or Albumasar (c. 787-886) was a prominent practicing Arabian astrologer. According to Al-Biruni, Abu Ma'shar likely used a translation of Vettius Valens as a basis for part of his work. The section on the basic meanings of the planets in this book is from the forthcoming translation of the ***Great Introduction*** from the Arabic by Dr. Benjamin Dykes, PhD. D. A translation of Abu Ma'shar's book on predictive techniques, ***On The Revolution of Nativities***, was recently published by Ben Dykes, and it contains a wealth of interpretive text on the planets applying to prediction.

Al-Biruni (973-1048?) in Afghanistan was an Arabian scholar and astrologer of Persian descent. He was a scholar and scientist, and wrote works on history, philosophy, mathematics, medicine, and of course astrology. His main astrological work, ***The Book of Instruction of the Elements of the Art of Astrology***, includes an explanation of arithmetic, geometry, trigonometry and astronomy along with the sections specific to astrology. According to Holden it is likely that his principal authority and source was Abu Ma'shar.

William Ramesey (1627-1676?) was an English physician and astrologer who focused on Elections and on Mundane astrology. His astrology textbook, ***Astrologia Restaurata, or Astrologie Restored***, is in four Books: a vindication of astrology, a general introduction, a text on Elections, and a text on Mundane. The excerpts I include here are from the second introductory book, and they are full of color and detail.

William Lilly (1602-1681) is the most famous English astrologer in history, and his classic textbook, ***Christian Astrology***, is arguably the greatest work on astrology written in the English language, and among the most important astrology texts of any era. Lilly was a practicing astrologer and is especially known for his mastery of horary astrology - book two of Christian Astrology is on horary and includes approximately 40 fully worked example charts. Lilly was widely read in the historical tradition, coming from the Greek and Arabic into the Latin, and his library included practically every important book on astrology then available. His work is firmly grounded in tradition and also includes his extensive practicing experience. Both the book ***Christian Astrology*** and Lilly's Autobiography are both well worth reading, and both are available in multiple editions.

As of this writing the source texts that I use here are in print and widely available in inexpensive editions, or will be published and available soon.

Reading the Traditional Texts

As you read the traditional texts I think you will find that they do not read like modern prose. The structure is different, and you need to go at a different pace and pay very careful attention. You need a different reading strategy to make sense of them.

To give you an example, the following quote from Abu Mashar on the planet Mars is a single sentence in the original source text.

[QUOTE FROM ABU MASHAR]

12 And he indicates youth, strength, mental sharpness, heat, fires, conflagration, every matter occurring suddenly, a king who has power and valor, cavalrymen, chief commanders, soldiers, the companions of the Sultan, oppression, coercion, war, killing, fighting, courage, hardiness, seeking glory, renown, and rank; the instruments of war, those entrusted with mobilizing wars, seeking retaliation, provoking discord, those craving groups and splitting apart, warring with one another, becoming a thief, digging, stealing, highway robbery, haughtiness, risk-taking, anger, regarding forbidden things as permissible, punishment, fetters, beating, imprisonment, restriction, running away, desertion, capture, prisoners, fear, conflict, injustice, anger, fury, recklessness, harshness, a coarseness of heart, foolishness, stubbornness, with scarce examination, haste, quickness in things, daring, bad in expression, ugliness of speech (and its coarseness and harshness), indecency of the tongue, revealing love and affection, glad tidings, extravagance in speech, [using] wiles in answering quickly [but with] repentance in it [afterwards], a scarcity of piety and scarcity of fidelity but an abundance of lying, slander, and debauchery; swearing false oaths, deception, cunning, bad works, a scarcity of good, the undermining of suitable things, an abundance of thought in matters, whims, independence of opinion from situation to situation but quickly going back, an insolent look, little shame, an abundance of trouble and

exertion, travels, exile, isolation, being a bad neighbor, fornication, ugly sexual intercourse, jokes, liveliness, the movement which happens at the time of a woman giving birth, the labor pains of a pregnant woman, the death of women in pregnancy, the cutting of a child in the womb, and the miscarriage of a fetus.

[END OF QUOTE]

This is not structured like what we would call a sentence or paragraph in modern prose. It is more like a long list or catalog, and not all of the meanings relate to each other.

In the section on Mars in this book I break this single sentence up into separate clauses on the page to make it easier for modern eyes to scan. If you are reading traditional texts for yourself you will often need to go through the text word by word, clause by clause, and not expect smooth, quick reading modern prose.

It is very important to read the traditional source texts SLOWLY. None of the sections included here are long, all of them are rich in meaning, and you will likely return to them again and again. You will see that there are a lot of similarities between the different authors, and together they are richer in meaning than they are separately. Overall there is a very remarkable consistency of meaning considering that the texts we are looking at here span a time frame of around 15 centuries.

Reading the source texts you will catalogs or lists of meanings that are not always related to each other. The task of digesting them, of coming up with the integrating factors, is something that needs to be done by the student. This is practically the inverse of the style of learning in modern astrology, which starts with single keywords and core concepts and then branches out from there. In traditional astrology you have the catalogs of varying attributes, and you have to distill out the integrating factors for yourself. Those integrating factors are not always simple and neat, nor are they easy to boil down to a few key concepts. It is worth resisting the urge to boil them down too far or make them too neat.

I find that, rather than having keyword summary concepts, the integrating factors are more like themes or clusters of meaning, where you will have several attributes having a common factor. I will discuss some of those common factors that I use, but I will put those after the source texts, so that you get a chance to wrestle with and confront them yourself.

There is another characteristic of the traditional texts that may take some getting used to. The meanings in the traditional texts are often extreme cases, either very bad or very good. You need to take that into account, and remember that most of the time planets are not that extreme in manifestation. You need to know how to weigh the extreme descriptions, and modify them according to their condition in a specific chart. A malefic needs to be extremely debilitated to be its worst, a benefic needs to be extremely strong and dignified to be its absolute best, and both extremes are rare.

The Source Texts - Introduction

With the first two astrologers, VettiusValens and Abu Mashar, I am including the complete texts of the sections in their books about the planets. For Al-Biruni and William Ramesey I am taking substantial excerpts, and with William Lilly I include the majority of his text.

I am including commentary by me after each of the sections of the text. Since the various source texts overlap in meaning quite a bit, generally I will not be repeating points covered in an earlier text. With this arrangement you can easily read the source texts by themselves without commentary.

At the end of each group of texts I will share some of my own thoughts on the planets and their attributes. The purpose of my interpretive comments is not to be definitive or inclusive, but to give some ideas for starting to think about them. Part of the purpose of this book is to give you an opportunity to work with drawing meaning from the source texts for yourself, and hopefully entice you to explore further within the original texts.

I comment the two earlier texts, Vettius Valens and Abu Mashar, more heavily than later authors since there is so much overlap in meaning. I will only comment on the later texts where a specific meaning stands out or needs clarification. For most of the examples, the sections from William Ramesey and William Lilly will have little or no commentary.

You will note that there is a great deal of overlap in the subjects assigned to the various planets. For example, knowledge and learning are attributed to Mercury, to the Sun, to Jupiter and to Saturn. Each of those relate to knowledge, yet each relates in a somewhat different way, with a different flavor. Some planets have a great deal of affinity in meaning, like Jupiter and the Sun. The planets Mercury and Venus take some of their meaning from being close to the Sun, so each overlaps in meaning with the Sun.

The Source Texts - Introduction

For many of the planets I will be including quotes from writers in the Platonist tradition. That will often add the meaning of each of the planets in a higher spiritual sense, where each planet fits in what you could call the divine economy. There is a spiritual dimension to the planets in Platonist tradition, and astrology in that sense becomes a link to the divine. Astrology is a religion in the root meaning of the term, re-ligare, re-linking us to divine unity and underlying order.

In my notes I will also comment on ways the traditional meaning differs from the modern, which can be quite significant. Part of learning traditional astrology involves setting aside some of the meanings from modern astrology that do not apply to traditional. To understand what a planet means you need to be clear on what it does not mean. I want to emphasize that this does not mean that modern meanings for the planets do not work, but that they are different in many cases from traditional meanings. If you wish to learn traditional astrology I think it is important to be clear on those differences.

The Moon - Source Texts

The Moon - Valens

The Moon, lit by the reflection of the sun's light and possessing a borrowed light, in a nativity indicates man's life, body, the mother, conception, <beauty>, appearance, sight, living together (i.e. legitimate marriage), nurture, the older brother, housekeeping, the queen, the mistress of the house, possessions, fortune, the city, the assembly of the people, gains, expenses, the household, voyages, travel and wanderings (it does not provide straight pathways because of Cancer).

The Moon rules the parts of the body as follows: the left eye, the stomach, the breasts, the breath, the spleen, the dura mater, the marrow (as a result it causes dropsy/moist syndromes).

Of materials it rules silver and glass. It is of the night sect, green in color and salty in taste.

[COMMENT]

All the main themes of the Moon are already here in one of the earliest surviving texts we have. The key point is the fact that the Moon's light is borrowed or reflected light from Sun; the Moon has no light of its own.

Moon is associated with the physical life and the body. The Moon is also our mortality, life within the changeable world where everything is born, grows, fades and dies like the Moon's phases. Moon is also the mother, woman, and anything to do with birth or rearing, or with woman's traditional roles. Being physical, Moon relates to possessions, physical things we own. This is likely related to the fact that fortune waxes and wanes like the Moon.

If Sun is the King then Moon is the common people in mundane astrology, and often relates to groups of people, assemblies.

Moon is also connected to voyages, traveling, moving - the Moon is the planet that moves most quickly through the sky. Regarding the reference to 'not providing straight pathways because of Cancer' - crabs move sideways.

Moon and other planets

Saturn and the Moon are beneficial, productive of money, estates, ship ownership, and profits from the deceased, especially if the Moon happens to be in the part of its orbit just following first visibility and has benefics in aspect. Then it causes association with the great, gifts, and the discomfiture of enemies. This combination, however, is unsteady with respect to possession, and with respect to women it is insecure and painful because of separations, hatred, and grief. It also produces bodily suffering, sudden fits, pains of the governing faculties and nerves, as well as the deaths of important figures.

[COMMENT]

The Moon is physical belongings in general, Saturn is related to landed property. Regarding profits from the deceased, Saturn is related to death, and we could have a connection here to waning then new Moon and death. Similarly, the Moon is the body, Saturn is suffering so we see bodily suffering. The Moon is fluctuating, and Saturn is related to separation, loss, death and grief. The mentions the emotional effect since the Moon is also fluctuating emotions.

We see association with the great;- Saturn is rulers, especially those in power, and the Moon is those who associate with the Saturnian ruler.

Jupiter and the Moon are good, acquisitive: they cause men to be masters of adornments and slaves, and they bestow distinguished offices and ranks. They cause men to benefit from women and distinguished individuals, to be treated well by family and children, and to be thought worthy of gifts and honors. They make treasurers, men who lend much, who are trusted, and who find treasures and become wealthy.

[COMMENT]

Jupiter is related to wealth, affluence and power, and slaves and adornments would be Moon qualities.

Adornment is related to the Moon as reflected light, appearance. The way that the way things look in Moonlight can be deceiving. There is also a glamorous and dreamlike quality to the appearance of things in Moonlight.

Men benefiting from women is related to Jupiter benefiting from the Moon. This is also people being well treated and valued. The connection with family and children is Lunar as is people in general, and being well thought of and honored in Jupiter.

Both Moon and Jupiter relate to belongings and treasure; put those two together and you get wealth.

Venus and the Moon are good with respect to rank, acquisitions, and the inception of business, but they are unsteady with respect to living together, friendships, and marriage, bringing rivalry and hostility, as well as ill-treatment and upset from relatives and friends. Likewise with respect to children and slaves, these stars are not good: they cause possessions to be fleeting and bring mental anguish.

[COMMENT]

Both Venus and Moon are related to relationships, especially women and families. Both, especially the Moon, are very unstable and fluctuating, they are fast moving planets. This describes fluctuating relationships between people. Any combination of these two is going to be fleeting, quickly changing. For stability you need one of the ponderous, slow-moving planets, Jupiter and Saturn

Mercury and the Moon are good with respect to the union and status of men and women, with respect to the power of speech and education, and concerning commerce and other enterprises. They make men who act in common, who are resourceful, experienced, inquisitive. They also cause men to advance by great expenditures, to be very changeable, not persevering in their activities or intentions for the future. <These men are> noble in the face of adversity, but are subject to ups and downs in their livelihood.

[COMMENT]

Mercury and Moon are both related to communication and commerce. Mercury adds being resourceful and inquisitive. Both being rapidly moving and fluctuating planets, you get references to rapidly changing situations or fluctuations, or lack of perseverance. Mercury particularly rules commerce, and Moon is related to physical belongings and wealth, hence fluctuations in livelihood.

The Sun and the Moon are good. They are productive of associations with the great and of high rank, as well as possession of estates, property, money, and adornment. These stars cause men to be successful in business enterprises and to receive profit. If the basis <of the nativity> is found to be great, men become leaders of cities, in charge of affairs, preeminent among the masses, gifted with a very high public image, munificent, governing, ruling, unsurpassed, and

45

possessing a kingly property and spirit. Those starting with a moderate/average fortune become lucky and are called blessed. The good, however, does not last for this type of person, because of the waning configuration of the Moon.

[COMMENT]

Sun adds the connection with greatness and high rank, somewhat similar to what we see with Jupiter or Saturn. Moon is repeatedly linked to businesses and wealth, and will benefit from good connections with the Sun. The reference to being great men and leaders are mostly connected with the Sun. The Moon adds an unstable, fluctuating quality that does not persevere.

The Moon - Abu Mashar

33 And as for the Moon, she is the luminary of the night, and her nature is cooling, moist, phlegmatic (and in her is incidental heat, because her glow is from the Sun), and she is light, suitable in every affair, craving joy and beauty of character, and being praised.

34 And she indicates the inception of all works, and kings, the nobles, good fortune in [one's] way of life, success in the things she wants, decency in religion, the higher sciences, wonders and sorcerers, an abundance of thought about things, and premonition; engineering, the science of lands and waters (and their assessment), calculation and accounting, and the weakness of reason.

35 And she indicates women who have nobility, and marriage, every pregnant woman, upbringing and its conditions, mothers, maternal aunts, wet nurses, and older sisters; and messengers, the postal service, reports, runaways, and lying and slander; [such a man is] a king with kings, a slave with slaves, and with every man he is like his nature; very forgetful, cowardly, without guile, cheerful towards people, honored among them, [but then] cast out from them, not concealing his secret.

36 And she indicates an abundance of illnesses, concerns with the mending of bodies, shaving the hair, and an abundance of food, [but] little sexual intercourse.

[COMMENT]

We have noted the Moon as reflection of the Sun. Phlegmatic is the humor associated with water, and is cold and moist.

Moon here shares some of the same group of attributes with Mercury - religion, sciences, sorcerers, engineering. Sorcery here might connote any magic that works on appearance since Moon has a lot to do with appearance, what we might think of as hypnosis or illusion. Weakness of reason - Moon is fluctuating and emotional, so any thought would be influenced by that - it ties in with the general association of Moon with instability. Moon also relates to speech, reports, gossip, slander, the sort of speech that spreads quickly through the common people, that fluctuates rapidly, arising and then fading as quickly. Rapidly moving Moon spreads the gossip through the common folk. We see connections with messengers, like with Mercury. Think of Moon as the quick-running courier who conveys things from planet to planet.

Moon's connection with women, marriage, pregnancy and motherhood including upbringing and any female relatives. The Moon is related to nurture, nourishing, so we see reference to abundance of food. The Moon is the planet to look at for issues with eating or indulgences relating to food.

Like Mercury, Moon varies according to which other planet it is relating to; it takes on the color and properties of aspecting planets and is easily influenced. She is a king with kings, a slave with slaves. Being a dependent and easily influenced, we see the Moon described as craving joy, beauty, praise. Think of Moon as reflecting the Sun's light, so it gets its worth from others, hence being praised, wanting to be thought beautiful. It is beauty as it is reflected in the eyes of others.

Some of the references are about Moon as socialization, groups of people; being cheery, relating to others, having an unstable reputation. The communication is also unstable, fluctuating, untrustworthy.

The Moon - Al-Biruni

NATURES OF THE PLANETS

Moon is cold and moist, sometimes moderate, changeable. Beneficent and maleficent. Female. Nocturnal. Salt or insipid, somewhat bitter. Blue and white or some deep colour not unmixed with reddish yellow, moderate brilliancy. Thickest, densest, moistest and lightest objects.

[COMMENT]

These are themes we have seen before - cold and moist, changeable. For the taste think of seawater or the taste of blood - most human body fluids are salty. Both of the lights, Moon and Sun, can be either benefic or malefic depending on condition.

BUILDINGS AND COUNTRIES

Moist places, underground or underwater brick-making, places to cool water, streams and roads with trees.

[COMMENT]

The connection here is mainly with water. The underground connection may have to do with Moon being associated with night and below, as opposed to Sun and above. It is also true that underground caverns can tend to get damp.

RELATIONS AND CONNECTIONS, FIGURE AND FACE

Mothers, maternal aunts, elder sisters, nurses. Clear white complexion, gait and figure erect, round face, long beard, eyebrows joined, teeth separate crooked at the points, good hair with locks.

DISPOSITION AND MANNERS

Simple, adaptable, a king among kings, a servant among servants, good-hearted, forgetful, loquacious, timid, reveals secrets, a lover of elegance, respected by people, cheerful, a lover of women, too anxious, not intellectually strong, much thought and talk.

[COMMENT]

Much of this has to do with the Moon changing according to the other planets it contacts.

ACTIVITIES, INSTINCTS AND MORALS

Lying, calumniation, over-anxious for health and comfort, generous in distributing food, too uxorious, levity in appropriate places, excellent spirits.

[COMMENT]

This is the Moon as fluctuating and untrustworthy combined with the Moon as health and comfort. Moon relates to love of luxury and physical sensation, and of pleasurable body activities like eating. The Moon rules emotions and fluctuates so it can be gay and joyous, but that can also fluctuate to moody and depressed.

CLASSES OF PEOPLE

Kings, nobles, noble matrons; celebrated, and wealthy citizens.

[COMMENT]

This is interesting since it associates the Moon with what are usually Solar sorts of connotations - royalty, fame, wealth. These associations are not as common in the tradition as a whole. It could mean being part of royal society.

RELIGIONS, PICTURES OF PLANETS

Adherents of the prevailing religion. Man with javelin in his right hand, in his left thirty, you would think there were three hundred, on his head a crown, seated in a chariot drawn by four horses.

TRADES AND PROFESSIONS

Engaged in business matters, missions, agencies, accounting; strenuous in religion and divine law, skill in all branches; practice of medicine, geometry, the higher sciences, measuring land and water; growing and cutting hair; selling food, silver rings and virgins, also indicates captivity, and prison for the deceptions of wizards.

[COMMENT]

Again we see the Moon associated with Mercurial sorts of activities like business, trade and accounting, and also various sciences. Many of the other connotations have to do with food, luxury, nourishing, sensation and physical enjoyment. Hair is mentioned as a part of the body that grows very quickly.

About prison for deception of wizards, this is the Moon as untrustworthy, but also the Moon as casting deceptive spells, being a sorcerer or witch.

The Moon - William Ramesey

She is neither fortunate nor unfortunate, but as she is placed and in configuration with either the Fortunes or Malevolents; she is most powerful in operation of all the other Planets, on Elementary bodies, by reason of their proximity to us, and her swiftness, by which she transfers the light and influence of all the superiors to us, by her configurations with them.

Moon Lady of the year, and strong in any Revolution, denotes there shall be no want of rain in its due season, both former and latter; men shall be generally healthy, fortunate, safe and punctual in all their actions and promises, especially if she be in reception with her dispositor, or good Aspects therewith, &c. but if she be weak and unfortunate, you are to judge the contrary.

She signifieth common people.

Of Herbs: Sea-tangle, Lunaria or the Moon-herb, Hyssop, Rosemary, Agnus-cactus, the herb Chista, Melon, Muskmelon, Gourd, Cucumber, Colwort, Cabbage, Endive, Mushrooms, Poppy, Lintseed, Rapeseed, and all such herbs as turn towards the Moon, and increase and decrease as she doth.

Of Trees and Plants: The Palm-tree, for that sends forth a twig every time the Moon riseth, and all such trees and plants as participate or sympathize with her, and are juicy and full of sap.

Of Birds: Goose, Swan, Duck, Divedapper, Moon-hen, and all Fowl using the water, Night-owl, Night-ravens, Bat, &c.

All Stones that are white and green, the Marchasite, the Crystal, the Senenite, and soft stones.

Of Minerals, Silver.

The Moon - William Ramesey

Of Fishes, Aelurus, whose eyes increase and decrease according to the course of the Moon, all fish of like nature; the Tortoise, Crab, Otter, Lobster, Cockle, Mussel, and all shell-fish; also the Eel, &c.

Of Beasts, such Beasts as use and delight in water, as the Otter, &c., and such as sympathize any wise with the Moon, as the Chameleon, Dog, Hog, Frog, Hind, Goat, Baboon, Panther, Cat, the Civet Cat, all monstrous beasts, Mice, Rats. Of the Baboons passions I forbear here to speak, since you have had it related in the chapter (on the Sun), being caused by the secret influence of Sol and Luna.

Of Places, Fountains, Fields, Sea-Ports, High-ways, Rivers, Deserts, Pools, Fish-Ponds, Bogs, Brooks, Docks, Springs, Common-shores, Wharves, &c.

Of Weather, according to her configuration with other planets, viz., with Saturn, cold, moist and cloudy weather, with Jupiter heat and temperate air, with Mars, wind and clouds; with the Sun according to the time of year; with Venus showers; with Mercury wind and rain.

Of Journeys, according as she is strong or weak, strengthened or debilitated.

Of Diseases, Megrims [Migraines], Frenzies, Apoplexies, Vertigos, Wind-cholic, Diseases in the Bladder, Testicles and left-side and in the liver of women, and members of Generation, Menstrues, Fluxes, cold Rhumes, Belchings, cold stomach, hurts in the left eyes of men and right of women, Sciatica, Surfeits, Coughs, Convulsions, Falling-sickness, Small-pox, Measles, and the Kings-evil [scrofula, tuberculosis].

The Moon - William Lilly

[NAME.] The Moon we find called by the Ancients, Lucina, Cynthia, Diana, Phoebe, Latona, Noctiluca, Proserpina; she is nearest to the Earth of all the Planets; her colour in the Element is vulgarly known:

[HOUSE.] She hath the Sign Cancer for her house, and Capricorn for her detriment; she is exalted in 3. Taurus, and hath her fall in 3. Scorpio.

[NATURE.] She is Feminine, Nocturnal Planet, Cold, Moist and Phlegmatic.

[MANNERS OR ACTIONS WHEN WELL PLACED OR DIGNIFIED.] She signifieth one of composed Manners, a soft, tender creature, a Lover of all honest and ingenious Sciences, a Searcher of, and Delighter in Novelties, naturally propense to frit and shift his Habitation, unsteadfast, wholly caring for the present Times, Timorous, Prodigal, and easily Frighted, however loving Peace, and to live free from the cares of this Life, if a Mechanic, the man learns many Occupations, and frequently will be tampering with many ways to trade in.

[WHEN ILL DIGNIFIED.] A mere Vagabond, idle Person, hating Labor, a Drunkard, a Sot, one of no Spirit or Forecast, delighting to live beggarly and carefly [carefree, carelessly], one content in no condition of Life, either good or ill.

[CORPORATURE.] She generally presenteth a man of fair stature, whitely coloured, the Face round, gray Eyes, and a little louring [dark, sullen]; much Hair both on the Head, Face, and other parts; usually one Eye a little larger then the other; short Hands and fleshy, the whole Body inclining to be fleshy, plump, corpulent and phlegmatic: if she be impeded of the Sun in a Nativity or Question, she usually signifies some blemish in, or near the Eye: a blemish near the Eye, if she be

54

impedited in Succedent Houses; in the Sight, if she be unfortunate in Angles and with fixed Stars, called Nebulose.

[QUALITIES OF MEN AND WOMEN.] She signifieth Queens, Countesses, Ladies, all manner of Women; as also the common People, Travelers, Pilgrims, Sailors, Fishermen, Fish-mongers, Brewers, Tapsters, Vintners, Letter-carriers, Coach-men, Huntsmen, Messengers, (some say the Pope's Legates) Mariners, Millers, Ale-wives, Maistors, Drunkards, Oister-wives, Fisher-women, Char-women, Tripe-women, and generally such Women as carry Commodities in the Streets; as also, Midwives, Nurses, &c, Hackney-men, Water-men, Water-bearers.

[SICKNESSE.] Apoplexies, Palsy, the Cholic, the Bellyache, Disease in the Left Side, Stones, the Bladder and members of Generation, the Menstries and Liver: in Women Dropsies, Fluxes of Belly, all cold Rheumatic Diseases, cold Stomach, the Gout in the Wrists and Feet, Sciatica, Cholic, Worms in Children and men, Rheums or Hurts in the Eyes, viz, in the Left of Men, and Right of Women: Sursets, rotten Coughs, Convulsion fits, the Falling sickness, Kings-evil, Apostems, smallpox and Measles.

[COLOURS AND SAVORS.] Of Colors the White, or pale Yellowish White, pale Green, or a little of the Silver-color. Of Savors, the Fresh, or without any flavor, such as is in Herbs before they be ripe, or such as do moisten the Brain, &c.

[HERBS, PLANTS AND TREES.] Those Herbs which are subject to the Moon have soft and thick juicy leaves, of a waterish or a little sweetish taste, they love to grow in watery places, and grow quickly into a juicy magnitude; and are, The Colwort, Cabbage, Melon, Gourd, Pompion, Onion, Mandrake, Poppy, Lettice, Rape, the Linden-tree, Mushrooms, Endine, all Trees or Herbs who have round, shady, great spreading Leaves, and are little Fruitful.

[BEASTS OR BIRDS.] All such Beasts, or the like, as live in the water; as Frogs, the Otter, Snails, &c. the Weasel, the Cunny, all Sea Fowl, Coockoo, Geese and Duck, the Night-Owl.

[FISHES.] The Oyster and Cockle, all Shell-fish, the Crab and Lobster, Tortoise, Eels.

[PLACES.] Fields, Fountains, Baths, Havens of the Sea, Highways and Desert places, Port Towns, Rivers, Fish-ponds, standing Pools, Boggy places, Common-shores, little Brooks, Springs.

[MINERALS.] Silver.

[STONES.] The Selenite, all soft Stones, Crystals.

[WEATHER.] With Saturn cold Air; with Jupiter Serene; with Mars Winds red Clouds; with the Sun according to the Season; with Venus and Mercury Showers and Winds.

[WINDS.] In Hermetical operation, she delighteth towards the North, and usually when she is the strongest Planet in the Scheme, viz. in any Lunation, she stirs up Wind, according to the nature of the Planet she next applies unto.

[ANGEL.] Gabriel.

[DAY OF THE WEEK.] Her day is Monday the first hour and the eight, after the rise of the Sun.

The Moon - General Notes

"This divinity then has the relation of nature and of a mother with respect to generation, or the sublunary region. For all things are convolved and co-increased by her when she increases; but are diminished when she diminishes. This Goddess, too, benevolently leads into light the unapparent productive principles of nature. She likewise gives perfection to souls through a life according to virtue; but imparts to mortal animals a restitution of form."

- Proclus, On the Theology of Plato
  Translated by Thomas Taylor

The Moon has a very special complex role to play in traditional astrology. It is the innermost planet, the one closest to the earth. In the traditional Chaldean order of the cosmos which we saw in the first section of this book, inside of the Moon's orbit is the sub-lunary world, the realm of the four elements, of rapid change and unpredictability. Outside of the Moon's orbit are the very regular and predictable spheres of the other planets, and outside of that is the unchanging world of the fixed stars. In this traditional model the Moon marks the boundary between ordered and disordered.

The Moon is the opposite or partner of the Sun. The Moon is the lesser light of night as the Sun is the greater light of day. When we consider Vettius Valens and the other source texts, the key point is the fact that the Moon's light is borrowed or reflected light from Sun; the Moon has no light of its own. As the Sun is hot and dry, so the Moon is cold and moist. After the Sun sets and it gets dark is when things cool off, and moisture starts to condense out of the air. Much of the Moon's meaning comes from its pairing with the Sun, and its having complementary characteristics. It is dark, it is cold and wet, especially wet, and it has only a cool reflected light. If the Sun is the King then the

Moon is the common people in mundane astrology, and often relates to groups of people, assemblies.

Moon is also related to appearance, the superficial. Our physical bodies are what we present to the world, the image or reflection we wish to present. This connects the Moon with sight and with appearance. The Moon has only the reflected light it receives from the Sun, and that light is unstable and changing. We see the rapid change of shape of the Moon monthly with its cycle of waxing and waning phases. The Moon comes to stand for all that is mutable, and also all that is periodic, cyclic. In cultures that live more closely in tune with the earth there is often a synchronization of the Moon's phases with women's menstrual cycles, so the Moon is related to women and to childbearing. The Moon is also related to emotional cycles. Our language has the words lunacy and lunatic to refer to the emotional influence of the Moon. Anecdotally, I have heard that emergency room calls in hospitals peak on the full Moon.

There is a special emphasis in traditional astrology on the Moon because of the speed with which it moves. The Moon acts as a sort of courier service that transfers the effects of the other planets from one to the other. With the Moon having this courier service role, conveying the effects of the other planets from one to another, it follows that the Moon itself is very strongly affected by the other planets it aspects, and reflects back some of their qualities. The Moon's job is to be affected by the other planets, and then to pass that on.

In any chart, especially in horary astrology, it is very important to look at the last aspect the Moon has made, and the next aspect it is about to make. The previous aspect is what has just happened, the next aspect is what is about to happen. Also important is the last aspect the Moon makes before changing sign, as that is the last of a series. The Moon's aspects makes things happen, and her aspects, one after the other, are a series of events. That is why the void of course Moon in horary traditionally means nothing much is going to happen. The Moon is also connected to voyages, traveling, moving, being the planet that moves most quickly through the sky.

The Moon is associated with the physical life and the body. It indicates people as physical beings. Since the Moon is physical life, the Moon is the first place to check whenever you are dealing with health issues. The Moon is the physical body while Sun is more like overall vitality and energy. The Moon is also our mortality, life within the changeable world where everything is born, grows, fades and dies like the Moon's phases. Moon is also the mother, woman, who gives of her body to create the physical bodies of her children. She rules anything to do with birth or rearing, or with the woman's traditional role in housekeeping. Being physical, the Moon also relates to possessions, physical things we own. This is likely related to the fact that fortune waxes and wanes like the Moon.

There is some overlap with meanings attributed to Mercury. Moon and Mercury together have a lot to do with how we use our minds, and both Moon and Mercury, which are the most distinctly mental of the planets, are fast moving, changeable, unstable and most influenced by those around them. Both planets are also couriers, messengers that convey things.

As a general principle it is worth noting that it is a mistake to try to neatly sort out and separate the planet's meanings and to assign various topics like thinking or possessions to a single planet. The meanings often overlap, although each planet does have its own distinct color and feel.

Mercury - Source Texts

Mercury - Valens

Mercury indicates education, letters, disputation, reasoning, brotherhood, interpretation, embassies, number, accounts, geometry, markets, youth, games, theft, association, communication, service, gain, discoveries, obedience, sport, wrestling, declamation, certification, supervision, weighing and measuring, the testing of coinage, hearing, versatility.

 It is the bestower of forethought and intelligence, the lord of brothers and of younger children, and the creator of all marketing and banking. In its own character, it makes temple builders, modelers, sculptors, doctors, secretaries, legal advisors, orators, philosophers, architects, musicians, prophets, diviners, augurs, dream interpreters, braiders, weavers, systematic physicians, those in charge of war and strategy, and those undertaking any unusual, systematic work in accounting or with reasoning.

Mercury makes weight lifters and mimes, those making their livelihood with displays of skill, deception, gambling, or sleight of hand. It also rules those skilled interpreters of the heavens, those who by using pleasure or winning charm, earn fame for their amazing feats—all for the sake of gain.

This star's effects go in many directions, depending on the changes of the zodiac and the interactions of the stars, and yields quite varied results: knowledge for some, selling for others, service for others, trade or teaching for others, farming or temple service or public <employment> for still others. To some it grants authority, rentals, labor contracting, rhythmical performance, the display of public service, the acquisition of personal attendants or the right of wearing temple-linen, robed in the luxury appropriate to gods or rulers.

As for the end result—Mercury will make everything capricious in outcome and quite disturbed. Even more, it causes those having this star in malefic signs or degrees to become even worse.

Of the parts of the body, it rules the hands, the shoulders, the fingers, the joints, the belly, the sense of hearing, the arteries, the intestines, the tongue. Of materials, it rules copper and all coins used in buying and selling—for the god makes exchanges. ...<It is blue in color, sharp in taste.>

[COMMENT] Mercury is one of the innermost planets, the second in order after the Moon. While the Moon represents infants, Mercury represents children, traditionally especially young boys. Mercury is capricious, disturbed, unstable, changing, and takes on the color of the planet it most closely aspects. Sport, games, wrestling, are related to Mercury as youth, having a kind of playfulness.

Mercury is strongly associated with language, education, writing, reasoning, communication and verbal arts, both spoken and written. There is a strong association with markets, commerce, banking. These are all about money and goods changing hands, so this is related to Mercury as messenger, errand-runner, who passes goods from one to another. There is an association with weighing and measuring, testing coinage. This is related to markets and commerce. Counting, weighing and measuring are also all related to language.

Valens - Mercury in Combination

[TEXT] **Mercury and the Sun** make adaptable men with many friends, those flexible and self-controlled men who spend their careers in public places. These stars make pure, sensible men, men of good judgment, lovers of beauty, learned men, initiates into divine matters, beneficent, fond of their associates, independent, braggarts. These men endure reversals nobly, but are ineffective, suffering ups and downs in their livelihoods, experiencing vicissitudes. They are not poverty-stricken, but find a success proportional to the basis of their nativities.

[COMMENT] - Mercury with the Sun emphasizes adaptability, flexibility, ability to deal with changing fortune.

[TEXT] **Mercury and the Moon** are good with respect to the union and status of men and women, with respect to the power of speech and education, and concerning commerce and other enterprises. They make men who act in common, who are resourceful, experienced, inquisitive. They also cause men to advance by great expenditures, to be very changeable, not persevering in their activities or intentions for the future. <These men are> noble in the face of adversity, but are subject to ups and downs in their livelihood.

[COMMENT] These are related to people working together, acting in common. Both Mercury and Moon to relate to communication. Both planets are changeable and fast moving so there is an unstable, up and down quality to this.

[TEXT] **Mercury and Mars** are not good. They cause hostility, lawsuits, reversals, malice, betrayals, wrongs from superiors or inferiors. These stars make some men athletic, martial, commanding, beneficent, inquisitive <of the occult>, getting a livelihood in a varied manner. They resort to forgery in order to embezzle, steal, and loot, and having fallen into debt and expenses, they bring on themselves infamy and hot pursuit. If the configuration is afflicted, men meet with accusations and imprisonment, and they suffer loss or confiscation of goods.

[COMMENT] Mercury with Mars is bad, and brings out the unstable, untrustworthy, sly and deceitful side of both planets.

[TEXT] **Venus and Mercury** are in harmony. They make men sociable and gracious, gregarious and hedonistic, paying attention to education and sensibility, receiving honors and gifts. For those of mediocre fortune, these stars bring about the receiving of goods, selling, and exchanges, and they bring a base livelihood. These stars make men unsteady and fickle with respect to women, changeable in their agreements <with them>.

[TEXT] **Jupiter and Mercury** are good, in harmony, and supervisory. They make men who are managers, overseers of affairs, in posts of trust and administration. They make men who are successful as secretaries and accountants and who are respected in education. These are approachable people with many friends, judged worthy of pay and stipends. If Jupiter and Mercury are found in operative signs, they make men discoverers of treasures, or moneylenders who profit from cash deposits.

[COMMENT] - Jupiter takes Mercury's skills and puts them in a management and administration role. This emphasizes the commerce and marketing side of Mercury

[TEXT] **Saturn and Mercury** are allies and productive of activities/employment. They do, however, bring slanders about religion, lawsuits, and debts, as well as disturbances about written matters and money. On the other hand, these stars make men who are not without resources and not unintelligent, with much experience and awareness, and who are curious, far-seeing scholars, seekers after mystic lore, revering the gods, but with much on their consciences.

[COMMENT] - Mercury plus Saturn gives intelligence plus depth and experience. The malefic side of both can be deceitful, nasty and slanderous.

Mercury - Abu Mashar

23 As for Mercury, his nature inclines to the natures of the planets and signs he combines with, [although] an equal balance of dryness and coldness is in him.

24 And he indicates childhood, younger brothers, and an affection for male and female servants (as well as wanting a lot of them).

25 And he indicates divinity, revelation to prophets, reason, logic, speech, reports, rumors and heeding them, science, belief, a good education, intelligence, cleverness, debate, the humanities, philosophy, presenting knowledge, calculation, surveying, the measurements of [both] higher and earthly things, the science of the stars, prediction, tracking [signs], augury, omens, augury by birds, skill in matters, wisdom, obscure books, linguistic style, eloquence, pleasantness of speech and its quickness of exposition, occupying oneself with the sciences, a craving for leadership and fame in them, reputation and praise because of them, and competition in them, in all things.

26 And he indicates writing poetry, writers, government agencies, the land-tax, injustices, slander, lying, falsehood, forged books, and an awareness of hidden secrets.

27 And he indicates a scarcity of joy and the corruption of assets.

28 He indicates assets, distribution, markets, businesses, buying and selling, taking and giving, partnership, disavowal, theft, lawsuits, cunning, deception, shrewdness, resentment, lying, deep thought, no one knows what is in his soul, and he does not reveal it to [anyone].

29 And he indicates wrestlers, enmity, serious damage from enemies, much fear of them, slaves, servants, quickness in works, crooked morals, fickleness, charm, pleasantness in speech, bringing something about, encouragement, obedience, endurance, sympathy, mercy, compassion, tranquility, a dignified manner, refraining from evil,

65

beauty of religion, obedience to God, invoking rights, preserving his brethren; cowardly, timid, fearful, a beautiful voice and knowledge of melodies.

30 And he indicates skillfulness of the hand, and different crafts, and proficiency in everything he undertakes, and a yearning for every consummate and complete work.

31 And he indicates cupping, and one working with razors and combs.

32 And he indicates springs of water, rivers, irrigation canals, prisons, the dead, and proficiency with riding animals.

[COMMENT]

There is an overlap with the meanings we saw in Valens. We see Mercury as cold and dry, easily influenced, related to childhood and siblings.

Here the emphasis on learning, education, and thinking, includes what we would call a spiritual dimension - divinity, prophecy, reading omens, tracking the stars. In traditional astrology Mercury would be the best candidate to be considered as ruling astrology.

Combine Language and commerce and you get government agencies, taxes, keeping records.

Again we see the heavy emphasis on commerce and business. With Mercury being two sided and unstable there is the element of cunning, deceptiveness, and also shrewdness. Mercury relates to both communication and keeping things private or hidden. That makes sense when you consider Mercury is the planet that spends more time hidden by the Sun than any other.

Mercury also has a craft side. There is skillfulness in language, but also skillfulness with the hands.

Mercury - Al-Biruni

[NATURES OF THE PLANETS] Mercury is moderately cold and dry, the latter predominant. Beneficent. Male and diurnal by nature, but takes on the characteristics of others near.

[BUILDINGS AND COUNTRIES] Bazaars and divans, mosques, houses of painters and bleachers and such as are near orchards, irrigation channels and springs.

[COMMENT] Mercury has a connection with houses of worship and of commerce, and also houses of crafters. We again see a connection with places near running water, specifically water in motion, like springs and irrigation channels.

[RELATIONS AND CONNECTIONS, FIGURE AND FACE] Younger brothers. Fine figure, complexion brown with a greenish tinge, handsome, narrow forehead, thick ears, good nose, eyebrows joined, wide mouth, small teeth, thin beard, fine long hair, well shaped long feet.

[DISPOSITION AND MANNERS] Sharp intelligence and understanding, affability, gentleness, open countenance, elegance, far-sightedness, changeable, deeply interested in business, eager for pleasure, keeps secrets, seeking friendship of people, longing for power, reputation and approval, preserves true friends and withdraws from bad ones, keeps away from trickery, strife, malevolence, bad-heartedness and discord.

[COMMENT] Again there is the mixed quality. There is the emphasis on intelligence and foresight, and the commerce emphasis. We see a streak of ambition, wanting power, honor and approval from others. Mixed in with these good qualities is the other side of discord, competition, strife and bad will. Mercury is a reliable friend in some situations, not trustworthy in others.

[ACTIVITIES, INSTINCTS AND MORALS] Teaching manners, theology, revelation and logic, eloquent, fine voice, good memory for stories, ruining prospects by too great anxiety and misfortunes, fearful of enemies, frivolous, eager to buy slaves and girls, busybody, calumnious, thieving, lying and falsifying.

[COMMENT] Communication, learning, theology and revelation show up again, and communication includes good voice, and the ability to tell stories and persuade. The unstable quality of Mercury gives anxiety, varying fortunes, and a fearfulness. The changeable quality also has a frivolous side to it, a negative untrustworthy side.

[CLASSES OF PEOPLE] Merchants, bankers, councilors, tax-collectors, slaves and wrestlers.

[RELIGIONS, PICTURES OF PLANETS] Disputants in all sects. Youth seated on a peacock, in his right hand a serpent and in the left a tablet which he keeps reading. Another picture: man seated on a throne, in his hand a book which he is reading, crowned, yellow and green robe.

[TRADES AND PROFESSIONS] Merchants, calculators and surveyors, astrologers, necromancers and fortune tellers, geometrician, philosopher, disputation, poetry, eloquence, manual dexterity and desire for perfection in everything, selling slaves, hides, books, coins; profession of barber, manufacture of combs.

[COMMENT] Themes of the professions are general commerce, practices that divine the future, and general communication including debating and disputing.

Mercury - William Ramesey

He is like an Hermaphrodite, participating of both sex; he is Masculine when joined by Conjunction or Aspect to a Masculine planet, Feminine when with a Feminine; good and fortunate when joined with Fortunes, bad and mischievous when joined to or with the Malevolents.

When Mercury is strong and Lord of the year, he signifies Merchants, Tradesmen, and all such as give their minds to learning Arts and Sciences, shall have a successful year; but if he be weak, judge the contrary.

Quality of Men when well dignified: Astrologers, Philosophers, Mathematicians, Secretaries, Diviners, Merchants, Sculptors, Poets, Advocates, School-masters, Orators, Embassadors, Commissioners, Attorneys, Ingenious Artificers, &c. and all learned men in general.

When ill placed and weak: Scriveners, Accomptants, Clerks, Solicitors, Thieves, Carriers, Messengers, Footmen, Usurers, Petty-foggers, &c.

He is Author of Wit, Fancy, Ingenuity, and Invention.

Of Herbs: the Herb Mercury, Five-leaved grass, Fumitory, Marjoram, Parsely, Pimpernel, and such as are of diverse colors, and mixed natures; they have chiefly relation to the brain and tongue, to dispel wind, to comfort the Spirits, and open obstructions; Adders-tongue, Lungwort, Dragonwort, Cubabs and all such herbs as are beneficial to the Muses and Divination, as Vervin, Hiera, Treacle, Diambra.

Of Trees: the Walnut tree, Filbert tree, Hazel, &c.

Of Birds: Those Birds that are Naturally witty, melodious and inconstant, as the Linnet, Nightingale, Black-bird, Thrush, the Bird Ibis, the Bird Porphyrio, Parrot, Swallow, Popinjay; Cockatoo, Crane, the Jack-Daw, Lark, the Bird Calandra.

Serpents and Adders.

Of Stones: the Emerald, Agates, Red marble, Topaz, and such as are of diverse colors, Millstone, Marchasite.

Of Fishes: the Trochius, the Fox-fish, the Mullet, the Pourcontrell, the Fork-fish.

Of Beasts: the Dog, and such as are of quick sense, ingenious, inconstant, swift, and such as are easily acquainted with man, Apes, Foxes, Weasels, the Hart and Mule, the Hare, the Civet-cat, Squirrel, Spider, the Hyena, &c.

Of Weather, he must principally be observed, the sign and season of the year; but usually he causes rain, hail-storms, sometimes thunder and lightning, according to the nature of the Planets in configuration with him.

Of Places: Schools, Common-Halls, Tennis Courts, Fairs, Ordinaries, Markets, Bowling-Alleys, Tradelinens-shops in a gentlemans-house, his Hall, &c. Studies, Libraries.

In Journey, he is according as he is in place and in Aspects with other Planets.

Of diseases: Vertigos, Lethargies, Madness, Frenzies, Diseases of the brain, Ptisick, Stammerings, Defects in the memory, Hoarseness, Dry-cough, the Hand and Feet-gout, all imperfections in the Fancy.

Mercury - William Lilly

[NAME.] He is called Hermes, Stilbon, Cyllenius, Archas. Mercury is the least of all the Planets, never distant from the Sun above 27.degrees; by which reason he is seldom visible to our sight.

[COLOUR.] He is of a dusky silver colour; his mean motion is 59 min. and 8 seconds; but he is sometimes so swift that he moveth one degree and 40.min. in a day, never more; so that you are not to marvel if you find him sometimes go 66. 68. 70. 80. 86. or 100. in a day: he is Stationary one day, and retrograde 24.dayes.

[HOUSE.] He hath Gemini and Virgo for his Houses, and is exalted in the 15. of Virgo: he receives detriment in Sagittarius and Pisces, his fall is in Pisces.

[NATURE.] We may not call him either Masculine or Feminine, for he is either the one or other as joined to any Planet; for if in Conjunction with a Masculine Planet, he becomes Masculine; if with a Feminine, then Feminine, but of his own nature he is cold and dry, and therefore Melancholy; with the good he is good, with the evil Planets ill.

[ELEMENTS.] In the Elements the Water; amongst the humours, the mixed, he rules the animal spirit: he is author of subtlety, tricks, devices, perjury, &c.

[MANNERS WHEN WELL PLACED.] Being well dignified, he represents a man of a subtle and politic brain, intellect, and cogitation; an excellent disputant or Logician, arguing with learning and discretion, and using much eloquence in his speech, a searcher into all kinds of Mysteries and Learning, sharp and witty, learning almost any thing without a Teacher; ambitious of being exquisite in every Science, desirous naturally of travel and seeing foreign parts: a man of an unwearied fancy, curious in the search of any occult knowledge; able by his own Genius to produce wonders; given to Divination and the more

71

secret knowledge; if he turn Merchant, no man exceeds him in a way of Trade or invention of new ways whereby to obtain wealth.

[MANNERS, WHEN ILL PLACED OR DIGNIFIED.] A troublesome wit, a kind of Frenetic man, his tongue and Pen against every man, wholly bent to spoil his estate and time in prating and trying nice conclusions to no purpose; a great liar, boaster, prattler, busybody, false, a tale-carrier, given to wicked ARTS, as Necromancy, and such like ungodly knowledges; easy of belief, an ass or very idiot, constant in no place or opinion, cheating and thieving every where; a news-monger, pretending all manner of knowledge, but guilty of no true or solid learning; a trifler; a mere frantic fellow; if he prove a Divine, then a mere verbal fellow, frothy of no judgment, easily perverted, constant in nothing but idle words and bragging.

[CORPORATURE,] Vulgarly he denotes one of an high stature and straight thin spare body, an high forehead and somewhat narrow long face, long nose; fair eyes, neither perfectly black or gray, thin lips and nose, little hair on the chin, but much on his head, and it a sad brown inclining to blackness; long arms, fingers and hands; his complexion like an Olive or Chestnut colour. You must more observe Mercury then all the Planets; for having any aspect to a Planet, he doth more usually partake of the influence of that Planet then any other doth: if with Saturn then heavy, with Jupiter more temperate, with Mars more rash, with Sun more genteel, with Venus more jesting, with Moon more shifter.

[ORIENTAL.] When he is Oriental, his complexion is honey colour, or like one well Sun-burnt; in the stature of his body not very high, but well jointed, small eyes, not much hair; in very truth, according to the height of body, very well composed, but still a defect in the complexion, viz. swarthy brown, and in the tongue, viz, all for his own ends.

[OCCIDENTAL.] When Occidental, a tawny visage, lank body, small slender limbs, hollow eyes, and sparkling and red or fiery; the whole frame of body inclining to dryness.

[QUALITY OF MEN AND PROFESSIONS.] He generally signifies all literated men, Philosophers, Mathematicians, Astrologians, Merchants, Secretaries, Scriveners, Diviners, Sculptors, Poets, Orators, Advocates, School-masters, Stationers, Printers, Exchangers of Money, Attorneys, Emperors, Embassadors, Commissioners, Clerks, Artificers, generally Accountants, Solicitors, sometimes Thieves, prattling muddy Ministers, busy Sectaries, and they unlearned; Grammarians, Tailors, Carriers, Messengers, Foot-men, Usurers.

[SICKNESS.] All Vertigos, Lethargies or giddiness in the Head, Madness, either Lightness, or any Disease of the Brain; Ptisick, all stammering and imperfection in the Tongue, vain and fond Imaginations, all defects in the Memory, Hoarseness, dry Coughs, too much abundance of Spittle, all snaffling and snuffling in the Head or Nose; the Hand and Feet Gout, Dumbness, Tongue-evil, all evils in the Fancy and intellectual parts.

[COLOURS AND SAVORS.] Mixed and new colors, the Gray mixed with Sky-color, such as is on the Neck of the Stock-dove, Linsie-woolsie colors, or consisting of many colors mixed in one. Of Savors an hodge-podge of all things together, so that no one can give it any true name; yet usually such as do quicken the Spirits, are subtle and penetrate, and in a manner insensible.

[HERBS AND PLANTS.] Herbs attributed to Mercury, are known by the various colour of the flower, and love sandy barren places, they bear their seed in husks or cobs, they smell rarely or subtilly, and have principal relation to the tongue, brain, lungs or memory; they dispel wind, and comfort the Animal spirits, and open obstructions. Beans, three leaved-grass, the Walnut and Walnut-tree; the Filbert-tree and Nut; the Elder-tree, Adders-tongue, Dragon-wort, Twopenny-grass,

73

Lungwort, Anniseeds, Cubebs, Marjoran. What herbs are used for the Muses and Divination, as Vervine, the Reed; of Drugs, Treacle, Hiera, Diambra.

[BEASTS.] The Hyaena, Ape, Fox, Squirrel, Weasel, the Spider, the Grayhound, the Hermaphrodite, being partaker of both sexes; all cunning creatures.

[BIRDS.] The Lynnet, the Parrot, the Popinian, the Swallow, the Pye, the Beetle, Pifinires, Locusts, Bees, Serpent, the Crane.

[FISHES.] The Forke-fish, Mullet.

[PLACES.] Tradesmens-shops, Markets, Fairs, Schools, Common Halls, Bowling-Alleys, Ordinaries, Tennis-Courts:

[MINERALS.] Quicksilver.

[STONES.] The Milestone, Marchasite or fire-stone, the Achates, Topaz, Vitro-il, all stones of divers colors.

[WINDS AND WEATHER.] He delights in Windy, Stormy and Violent, Boisterous Weather, and stirs up that Wind which the Planet signifies to which he applies; sometimes Rain, at other times Hail, Lightning, Thunder and Tempests— in hot Countries Earthquakes, but this must be observed really from the Sign and Season of the year.

[ORB.] His Orb is seven degrees before and after any aspect.

[ANGEL.] His Angel is named Raphael.

[DAY OF THE WEEK.] He governeth Wednesday, the first hour thereof, and the eight. His Friends are Jupiter, Venus, Saturn and his Enemies all the other Planets.

Mercury - General Notes

"Next to the Moon is Mercury, who is the cause of symmetry to all mundane natures, having the relation of reason to things in generation... This deity is the inspective guardian of gymnastic exercises; and hence *hermae*, or carved statues of Mercury were placed in the Palaestrae; of music, and hence he is honored as the lyrist among the celestial constellations; and of disciplines, because the invention of geometry, reasoning and discourse is referred to this God. He presides, therefore, over every species of discipline, leading us to an intelligible essence from this mortal abode, governing the different herds of souls, and dispersing the sleep and oblivion with which they are oppressed. He is likewise the supplier of recollection, the end of which is a genuine intellectual apprehension of divine natures."

- Proclus, On the Theology of Plato
  Translated by Thomas Taylor

Mercury is the most slippery, the most elusive planet, the most difficult to pin down and get a handle on. Like quicksilver, Mercury is a shape shifter. Mercury is also hermaphrodite, bisexual or non-sexual like children, or switching sexes depending on its position. All of the other planets come in pairs. There are two lights, two benefics, two malefics. Mercury is the exception.

House-wise, Mercury has its Joy in the first house, where the Ascendant is, right on the border of the horizon. The border is where consciousness happens. Mercury is a mediator, a messenger, a trader, exchanging across the border. Mercury is liminal, on a border, crossing the border, and in some ways Mercury is related to the border itself.

Without Mercury there is no awareness, nothing we would recognize as consciousness. As consciousness, Mercury goes in multiple directions. It can be outward focused, it can be inward focused, and convey information back and forth.

Mercury - General Notes

Mercury the messenger conveys news and information, but also convey goods and services, so we see the association with commerce, business, marketing, and money as a medium of exchange. Mercury is not so much the goods themselves but the act of exchanging them and the markets where the exchange takes place.

Mercury never gets very far from the Sun - its maximum distance is around 29 degrees - so it spends a lot of time going in and out of visibility. It also goes retrograde 3 or 4 times a year for around 3 weeks at a time. Its movement is rapidly changing and very unstable. Mercury conceals but also reveals, goes into and out of hiding, goes rapidly back and forth. Given this closeness there is a connection between Mercury and the Sun, and that leads to some overlap in their meaning. Mercury is conveying what comes from the Sun, and there is a connection between the Sun, consciousness and communication.

Like the Moon, another planet which is rapidly changing and unstable, Mercury takes on the color of whatever planets most closely aspect it. The two are rapidly changing in different ways. The Moon moves rapidly in a single direction but has phases, waxing and waning. Mercury's change consists of rapidly moving back and forth, frequently changing directions, and also going behind the Sun and out of visibility, then re-emerging on the other side, pausing and going back the other directions. The Moon's phase movement is a waxing and waning, Mercury's phase movement is an oscillation, more like a pendulum.

There is an association of Mercury with deception, gambling, slight of hand. Many of the planets have two sides, but for Mercury that two-sidedness is near the center of its meaning. Mercury is truth or falsehood, revealing or deceiving. These are both qualities of language and how it can be used. You really can't have falsehood or deception without language. It is a whole other level of consciousness, and falsehood implies a lack of correspondence between language and other levels of experience.

There also can be no self-consciousness without language, so Mercury is necessary for any sort of self-awareness, any sort of analytical consciousness, any consciousness that ponders, measures, compares, relates. There is a double-sidedness to language, to thinking, to consciousness, and to Mercury. On its lowest level Mercury can be deception, cheating, sleight of hand, manipulation. On its very highest level Mercury touches on the Logos, the creative word which is used by God/the Gods to create. Mercury is related to Thoth and Hermes, scribe of the Gods, god of wisdom. Creating, naming and language are all closely linked.

Venus - Source Texts

Venus - Valens

Venus is desire and love. It indicates the mother and nurture. It makes priesthoods, school superintendencies, high offices with the right to wear a gold ring or a crown, cheerfulness, friendship, companionship, the acquisition of property, the purchase of ornaments, agreements on favorable terms, marriages, pure trades, fine voices, a taste for music, sweet singing, beauty, painting, mixing of colors both in embroidery, dyeing, and unguent making. <Venus makes> the inventors and masters of these crafts, as well as craftsmanship or trade, and work in emeralds, precious stones, and ivory. Within its terms and degrees in the zodiac,

Venus causes men to be gold-spinners, gold workers, barbers, and people fond of cleanliness and toys. It bestows the office of supervisor of weights and measures, the standards of weights and measures, markets, factories, the giving and receiving <of gifts>, laughter, good cheer, ornamentation, and hunting in moist places. Venus gives benefits from royal women or from one's own, and it brings very high rank when it operates in such affairs,

Of the parts of the body, it rules the neck, the face, the lips, the sense of smell, the front parts from the feet to the head, the parts of intercourse; of the inner parts it rules the lungs. It is a recipient of support from others and of pleasure. Of materials it rules precious stones and fancy jewelry. Of fruits it rules the olive. It is of the night sect, white in color, very greasy in taste.

[COMMENT]

Many of the main themes for Venus are related to beauty, to women and to desire, including love and sex. There is an overlap with the Moon here concerning women and their roles including nurture.

We also see an overlap with the other benefic Jupiter, and also with the Sun since Venus is so close to the Sun. There is an association with priesthood & high offices. Valens mentions the 'right to wear a gold ring or crown', so there is an emphasis on jewelry, beauty and decoration with the high office.

Venus relates to bringing people together, so we see personal traits that are pleasant and attractive - cheefulness, friendship, social events, laughter, good cheer.

There is an association with acquisition of property and purchase of ornaments. This is related to wealth, and with a decorative property. We see an overlap with Mercury, with Venus being supervisor of measuring.

Venus and Other Planets

Saturn and Venus act harmoniously with respect to activities/employment: they promote success with respect to entanglements and marriage, agreeing and beneficial only for a time, not to the end. Indeed they cause abuse, divorces, inconstancy, and death, often entangling men with the base-born and the lowly, and causing them to fall into harm and lawsuits.

[COMMENT] Saturn has a mostly negative effect on Venus despite the opening sentence about acting harmoniously; this is only for a time, not to the end. You have the kinds of problems that come with bad relationships like abuse and inconstancy, and with marriages failing - divorces, lawsuits, even death.

Jupiter and Venus are good, in harmony, productive of rank and profits, bringing new acquisitions, gifts, adornments, control over slaves, rulerships, the begetting of children, high priesthoods, preeminence among the masses, honors of garlands and gold crowns. These stars make men who are worthy of statues and images, but they also make them subject to ups and downs with respect to marriages and children.

[COMMENT] The good fortune and power of Jupiter mixes here with the adornment and beauty of Venus. Jupiter's palaces just got prettier and more gilded, more decorated. Interestingly there is the effect of swings of fortune in the Venusian areas of marriage and children.

Venus and the Sun are in harmony, glorious, bestowers of good. They cause the association of male and female, they bring gifts and conveyances, and make men successful in their enterprises. Occasionally they make those men who take on popular leadership or trusts, those who are in charge of foreign/secure places, those thought worthy of stipends. These men, however, are not without grief with respect to wife and children, especially if Venus is setting.

[COMMENT] There is the magnanimous, powerful and generous effect of the Sun, and this has a good effect on male/female relationships. Again we have the note about problems with wife and children depending on the condition of Venus. Venus in several of these combinations adds an unstable, varying quality; it is not a very strong planet.

It is very important to note male/female relationships are associated here with Venus and Sun, not with Venus and Mars. Relationship itself is very much a Venusian theme.

Venus and the Moon are good with respect to rank, acquisitions, and the inception of business, but they are unsteady with respect to living together, friendships, and marriage, bringing rivalry and hostility, as well as ill-treatment and upset from relatives and friends. Likewise with respect to children and slaves, these stars are not good: they cause possessions to be fleeting and bring mental anguish.

[COMMENT] Again we have the emphasis on things being unsteady and fleeting - neither Moon nor Venus are slow and stable planets.

Venus and Mars are at odds. They make men unsteady and weak of mind; they cause rivalry and murder; they cause men to have many friends, but to be blameworthy, shameless, fickle, and equally prone to intercourse with men or women; to be malicious, and plotters of murder by poison. These stars cause men to remain with neither the good nor the bad, to be slandered and reviled because of their friendships, to be spendthrift, flitting from one occupation to another, to be eager for many things, to be wronged by women and because of them to suffer crises, upsets, and debts.

[COMMENT] We see very little emphasis on man/woman relationships. The mention of sex with men or women sounds like indiscriminate sex with little regard for relationships. Most of these attributes here are negative, undependable, unreliable, and it is describing people who are untrustworthy and create problems in relationship. Venus and Mars do not complement here; rather, it is more like Mars has a corrupting effect on Venus.

Venus and Mercury are in harmony. They make men sociable and gracious, gregarious and hedonistic, paying attention to education and sensibility, receiving honors and gifts. For those of mediocre fortune, these stars bring about the receiving of goods, selling, and exchanges, and they bring a base livelihood. These stars make men unsteady and fickle with respect to women, changeable in their agreements <with them>.

[COMMENT] Mercury and Venus here complement each other's social quality. Again we have them being unsteady and unreliable, which is a theme we see with both Mercury and Venus separately; the reliable planets are larger, like the Sun, and the large, slower moving Jupiter and Saturn. Moon, Mercury, and Venus are all fast-moving and two of them are frequently retrograde, so each has an unsteady and unreliable quality.

Venus - Abu Mashar

19 As for Venus, her nature is cooling, moist, phlegmatic, temperate, a fortune.

20 She indicates women, the mother, younger sisters, cleanliness, clothing, ornaments, gold and silver, graciousness towards close friends, conceit, vanity, haughtiness, boasting, the love of wealth and entertainment, laughter, adornment, joy, delight, dancing, playing horns, plucking the strings of the oud, weddings, perfume and good-smelling things, gentleness in composing melodies, playing backgammon and chess, idleness, casting off [restraint], going too far [in what is bad], buffoonery, occupying oneself with men and children in fornication, and every male or female fornicator, or male or female singer, or one playing types of instruments; and much swearing of oaths (and lying), wine, honey, drinking sweet intoxicants, having sex in various ways, as well as intercourse in the rear and lesbianism.

21 And she indicates a love for children and a love of people, and showing love towards them, tranquility towards everyone, tolerance, generosity, kindliness, liberality, freedom, a good character, beauty and handsomeness, ingratiation, reception, brightness, splendor, pleasantness of speech, the feminine, flirtation, passion, ridicule, wishing good health, strength of the body (but weakness of the soul), much flesh in bodies, an abundance of craving for everything, joy in everything, making demands for every thing (being eager for it).

22 And she indicates [different] types of clean, admirable crafts and works, stringing garlands and decorating them, wearing crowns, dyes and dyers, sewing, houses of worship, virtue, adhering to religion, performing devotions, justice, fairness, scales and measuring, a love of markets and being in them, business, and selling good-smelling things.

[COMMENT]

Not surprisingly these attributes are mostly in line with what we saw in Valens. There is a heavier emphasis in Abu Ma'shar on pleasure, pastimes and indulgence, especially all varieties of sexual indulgence.

There is abundance as in Jupiter, but it is more about abundance of pleasure and of beautiful or pleasant objects and pastimes. The aesthetic quality predominates over the quality of just wealth as abundance of money. Money and wealth show up with multiple planets; we see Jupiter associated with good fortune including financial fortune, and Mercury is related to everything to do with money, commerce, trading, business, buying and selling, while Venus relates to buying beautiful, decorative Venusian things.

Venus - Al-Biruni

[OVERALL COMMENT] These descriptions are in line with what we have seen in the prior authors; I think there are no real new meanings needing comment.

NATURES OF THE PLANETS

Venus is moderately cold and moist, especially the latter. The lesser benefic. Female. Nocturnal. Fat and sweet flavor. Pure white tending to straw color, shining, according to some greenish. Most pungent, most agreeable and delicious, most beautiful, softest and ripest things.

BUILDINGS

Lofty houses, vessels(roads) which hold much water, places of worship.

RELATIONS AND CONNECTIONS, FIGURE AND FACE

Wives, mothers, sisters, uterine kindred, delicate child. Fine round face, reddish-white complexion, double chin, fat cheeks, not too fat, fine eyes, the black larger than the white; small teeth, handsome neck, medium tall, short fingers, thick calves.

DISPOSITION AND MANNERS

Good disposition, handsome face, good-natured inclined to love and sensuality, friendliness, generosity, tenderness to children and friends, pride, joy, patience.

ACTIVITIES, INSTINCTS AND MORALS

Lazy, laughing, jesting, dancing, fond of wine, chess, draughts, cheating, takes pleasure in everything, not quarrelsome, a sodomite or given to excessive venery, well-spoken, fond of perfume, ornaments, song, gold, silver, fine clothes.

CLASSES OF PEOPLE

Nobles, plutocrats, queens courtesans, adulterers and their children.

RELIGIONS, PICTURES OF PLANETS

Islam. Woman on a camel holding a lute which she is playing; another picture: woman seated her hair unloosened the locks in her left hand, in the right a mirror in which she keeps looking, dressed in yellowish green, with a necklace, bells, bracelets and ankles.

TRADES AND PROFESSIONS

Works of beauty and magnificence, fond of bazaars, commerce, measuring by weight, length and bulk; dealing in pictures and colors, goldsmiths work, tailoring, manufacturing perfumes, dealing in pearls, gold and silver, ornaments, musk, white and green clothes, maker of crowns and diadems, accompanying singing, composing songs, playing the lute, feasts, games and gaming.

Venus - William Ramesey

I come now to Venus, who is next under Sol; she is the lesser Fortune, transparent, bright and shining; she is very well known by the Country people by the name of the Evening Star, when she sets after the Sun; and she is sometimes by them called the morning Star when she riseth before the Sun, Feminine and Nocturnal. And again, by some she is called the Shepherds Star.

When she is Lady of the year in any Revolution, and essentially dignified, the year will be advantageous unto women, who shall generally be free from infirmities, and mischiefs; they shall love and delight in the society of their Husbands, shall be fruitful, easily conceive and bring forth; the people shall also generally thrive and be prosperous, shall delight themselves in recreations, sports, feastings, mirth, and jollities, and all pleasure whatsoever; also in fine apparel; but if she be weak, judge the contrary.

Quality of Men when well placed: Musicians in general, Gamesters, and what Game soever it be, Embroiderers, Jewelers, Linnen-Drapers, Perfumers, Picture-Drawers, Engravers, Mercers, Silkmen, and all such Occupations as serve to the adorning of women, &c. Women, Wives, Mothers, Virgins, &c.

When ill placed or weak: Fiddlers, Pipers, ordinary Painters, Seamsters, Glovers, Womens-Tailors, Upholsterers, &c.

She is author of voluptuousness and pleasure.

Delightful, pleasant, toothsome, sweet savors.

All such herbs and plants as are odoriferous, pleasant, sweet and delectable, and such as invite to Venery, viz., the Satyrian, Daffodil, Cuckoo-Pintle, Maiden-hair, the Violet, Valerian, Vervin Thyme, the Rose, Lilly, &c. All such spices as are fragrant and sweet, &c.

Venus - William Ramesey

Trees and Perfumes: The Fig-tree, Pomegranate, the Cypress, sweet Apple-tree, Pear-tree, the Myrtle-tree, Walnut, Almond-tree, Peach, Apricots, the Raisin-tree or vine, Turpentine tree, the wild Ash-tree, &c. And of Perfumes, Ambergris, Musk, Civet, the Gum Ladanum, and all such sweet Perfumes, Frankincense, &c.

Of Birds, the Swan, Water-wag-tail, Swallow, Pelican, Nightingale, Pigeon, Sparrow, Turtle-Dove, Stock-Dove, Crow, the Eagle; because as the Egyptian report, it will come to the Male (if called) after she hath been trod thirteen times in a day, the Partridge, Thrush, Black-bird, Wren, &c.

Of Stones, the Beryl, Chrysolite, Emerald, Sapphire, Green Jasper, Corneola, Aetites, the Lazul, Coral, Alabaster Marble.

Of Minerals, Copper, Brass, and sometimes Silver, &c.

Of Fishes, the Pylchard, Gilthead, the Whiting, Crab, Tithymallus, Dolphin.

All such Animals as are of a strong love, delicious or luxurious; the Dog, Cony, Sheep, Goat, Bull, Calf, Panther and Hart.

Weather, she denotes gentle showers in Winter, and temperate heat in Summer.

In Journeys, she causes good success, mirth, and sport by the way.

Of Diseases, Cold and Moist Diseases, such as happen in the members of generation, veins, bladder, back, belly, navel, matrix, the Running of the reins, Gonorrhea Pox, both French and Neapolitan, Priapism, Surfeits, the Pissing Disease; weakness in the reins and members of generation, all strains by over much excess of lust.

Venus - William Lilly

[NAME.] After the Sun succeedeth Venus; who is sometimes called Cytherea, Aphrodite, Phosphoros, Vesperugo, Ericina.

[COLOUR IN THE ELEMENT.) She is a bright shining colour, and is well known amongst the vulgar by the name of the evening Star or Hesperus; and that is when she appears after the Sun is set: common people call her the morning Star, and the learned Lucifer, when she is seen long before the rising of the Sun.

[MOTION.] Her mean motion is 59 min. and 8 seconds: her diurnal motion is sometimes 62 min. a day 64.65.66.or 70.74.76.minutes; but 82 min. she never exceedeth.

[LATITUDE.] Her greatest North or South latitude is 9 degr. and two mm. In February 1843. she had eight degr. and 36 min. for her North latitude.

[HOUSES.] She hath Taurus and Libra for her houses, she is exalted in 27 Pisces, she receiveth detriment In Aries and Scorpio, and hath her fall In 27 Virgo.

[TRIPLICITY.] She governeth the Earthly Triplicity by day viz. Taurus, Virgo, Capricorn; she is two days stationary before retrogradation, and so many before direction, and doth usually continue retrograde 42 days.

[ELEMENT, NATURE.] She Is a Feminine Planet, temperately Cold and Moist, Nocturnal, the lesser Fortune, author of Mirth and Jollity; the elements, the Air and Water are Venereal; In the Humours, Phlegm with Blood, with Spirit, and Genital seed.

[MANNERS & LOVING QUALITY WHEN WELL PLACED.] She signifies a quiet man, not given to Law, Quarrel or Wrangling, not Vicious, Pleasant, Neat and Spruce, Loving Mirth in his words and actions, cleanly in Apparel, rather Drinking much then Gluttonous, prone to Venery, oft entangles in Love-matters, Zealous in their affections, Musical, delighting in Baths, and all honest merry Meetings, or Masques and Stage-plays, easy of Belief, and not given to Labour, or take any Pains, a Company-keeper, Cheerful, nothing Mistrustful, a right virtuous Man or Woman, oft had in some Jealousy, yet no cause for it.

[WHEN ILL.] Then he is Riotous, Expensive, wholly given to Looseness and Lewd companies of Women, nothing regarding his Reputation, coveting unlawful Beds, Incestuous, an Adulterer; Fanatical, a mere Skip-jack, of no Faith, no Repute, no Credit; spending his Means in Ale-houses, Taverns, and amongst Scandalous, Loose people; a mean Lazy companion, nothing careful of the things of this Life, or any thing Religious; a mere Atheist and natural man.

[CORPORATURE.] A man of fair, but not tall Stature, his Complexion, being white, tending to a little darkness, which makes him more Lovely; very fair Lovely Eyes, and a little black; a round Face, and not large, fair Hair, smooth, and plenty of it, and it usually of a light brown colour, a lovely Mouth and cherry Lips, the Face pretty fleshy, a rolling wandering Eye, a Body very delightful, Lovely and exceeding well shaped, one desirous of Trimming and making himself neat and complete both in Clothes and Body, a love dimple in his Cheeks, a steadfast Eye, and full amorous enticements.

[ORIENTAL.] When Oriental the Body inclines to tallness; or a kind of upright straightness in Person, not corpulent or very tall, but neatly composed. A right Venerian person, is such as we say, is a pretty, complete, handsome Man or Woman.

[OCCIDENTAL.] When she is Occidental, the Man is of more short stature, yet very decent and comely in Shape and Form, well liked of all.

[QUALITIES OF MEN & THEIR PROFESSIONS.] Musicians, Gamesters, Silk-men, Mercers, Linen-Drapers, Painters, Jewelers, Players, Lapidaries, Embroiderers, Women-tailors, Wives, Mothers, Virgins, Choristers, Fiddlers, Pipers, when joined with Moon, Ballad Singers, Perfumers, Seamstresses, Picture-drawers, Gravers, Upholsterers, Limners, Glovers, all such as sell those Commodities which adorn Women either, in Body (as Clothes) or in Face, (as Complexion-waters.)

[SICKNESS.] Diseases by her signified, are principally in the Matrix and members of Generation; in the reins, belly, back, navel and those parts; the Genorrex or running of the Reins, French or Spanish Pox; any disease arising by inordinate lust. Priapism, impotency in generation, Hernias & the Diabetes or pissing disease.

[SAVORS. AND COLOURS.] In colors she signifieth White, or milky Sky-color mixed with brown, or a little Green. In Savors she delights in that which is pleasant and toothsome; usually in moist and sweet, or what is very delectable; in smells what is unctious and Aromatical, and incites to wantonness.

[HERBS AND PLANTS.] Myrtle always green; all herbs which she governeth have a sweet flavor, a pleasant smell; a white flower; of a gentle humor, whose leaves are smooth and not jagged. She governeth the Lilly white and yellow, and the Lilly of the Valley, and of the Water. The Satyrion or Cuckoe-pintle, Maidenhair, Violet; the white and yellow Daffadil.

[TREES.] Sweet Apples, the white Rose, the Fig, the white Sycamore; wild Ash, Turpentine-tree, Olive, Sweet Oranges, Mugwort, Ladies-mantle, Sanicle-Baim, Veryin, Walnuts, Almonds, Millet, Valerian, Thyme, Ambre, Ladanum, Civet or Musk, Corriander, French Wheat, Peaches, Apricots, Plums, Raisins.

[BEASTS.] The Hart, the Panther, small cattle, Coney, the Calf, the Goat.

[BIRDS.] Stockdove, Wagtail, the Sparrow, Hen, the Nightingale, the Thrush, Pelican, Partridge, Ficedula, a little Bird Feeding on Grapes; the Wren, Eagles, the Swan, the Swallow, the Owse or Black Bird, the Pye.

[FISHES.] The Dolphin.

[PLACES.] Gardens, Fountains, Bride-chambers, fair lodgings, Beds, Hangings, Dancing-Schools, Wardrobes.

[METALS AND MINERALS, STONES.] Copper, especially the Corinthian and White; Brass, all Lattenware. Cornelian, the sky-coloured Sapphire, white and red Coral, Margalite, Alabaster, Lapis Luzuli because it expels Melancholy, the Beryl, Chrysolite.

[WINDE AND WEATHER.] She governeth the South-wind being hot and moist; in the temperament of the Air, she ruleth the Etesia; she foretelleth in Summer, Serenity or clear weather; in Winter, rain or snow.

[ORB.] Her Orb is 7. before and after any aspect of hers.

[ANGEL.] Her Angel is Anael.

[DAY OF THE WEEK.] Her day of the week Friday, of which she rules the first and eighth hour; and in conception the first Month. Her Friends are all the Planets except Saturn.

Venus - General Notes

"Venus, then, is the temperament of the celestial gods, and the friendship and union, by which their harmony subsists; for as she is proximate to the sun, in conjunction with whom she revolves, she fills the heavens with the best temperament, gives fertility to the earth, and is the source of perpetuity to the generation of animals. And of all this the sovereign sun is the primary cause: but Venus concurs in her operations with this divinity; alluring our souls with pleasure, and diffusing from aether, delightful and incorruptible splendours on the earth, far superior to the brightest refulgence of gold."

- Julian's Oration to the Sun, translated by Thomas Taylor

There are several characteristically Venus themes, and they intertwine nicely and harmoniously. Start with the very first sentence of Valens, as I think there is a lot in there. *Venus is desire and Love.* Combine that with Venus being related to woman and all things feminine, and you have the core of her meanings.

Venus is the planet of love and sex, allure, attraction, magnetism, desire. All of these are forces drawing things together, or perhaps all different expressions of a single force we name Venusian. Venus is binding things together by allure; it's not quite just beauty and not quite just lust, but those two are aspects of Venus. Venus also relates t beauty in the highest sense, and this is not confined to the superficial beauty of appearance. It brings together, harmonizes, blends, lends proportion and ease.

Related to being alluring and attractive, the meanings of Venus include aesthetics, beauty, decoration. Venusian qualities are well proportioned, harmonizing well, going together well. Venus helps to bind us together, and in human relations this can include things like politeness, good manners, good social graces.

Venus - General Notes

Venus is related to pleasure, enjoyment, and indulgence of all kinds. This can be physical and sensual pleasures, and it can be pleasure and satisfaction in other senses also. There can be a mental pleasure and enjoyment from pleasing, harmonious, well balanced thought.

Since Venus is strongly connected to women, you see some mention of nurture, child birth and rearing, but they are more emphasized with the Moon. The two feminine planets Venus and Moon both have a lot to do with physical creation and its beauty, of taking ideas and concepts and giving them flesh, and this is most beautiful and complete when the flesh embodies a high spiritual idea. This gives Venus a strong connection to the arts - music, dancing, painting, sewing, embroidery, jewelry. Venus is most strongly associated with decorative arts.

The connection of Venus with wealth, or with high offices and honors, are minor themes that show up in Valens, the earliest writer, but don't continue on into the later texts. By the time of Lilly they are mostly gone. Venus as related to wealth is not a main emphasis as it is in modern astrology. Regarding connection with wealth there is a lot of overlap between planets; you see such references to wealth with Saturn, Jupiter, the Sun, the Moon and also with Mercury.

In a higher Platonic sense, Venus as beauty, magnetism, and attractiveness, all point to a pure and divine quality. What we are ultimately attracted to in Venus is the source or principle of Beauty and Love which is a link right to the heart of the Divine. The magnificent Platonic dialog Symposium is a very good meditation on Love, Beauty and attraction and its different levels.

Like all the planets, Venus has a positive and a negative side, and we have just considered the highest, most benefic connection of Venus with divinity. Where Venus becomes malefic and negative is where that attraction becomes fixated or trapped in something lower, where higher is sacrificed to lower than the other way around. Then love deteriorates, and sexual interaction becomes exploitation, love for pleasure becomes gluttony, love for beauty becomes fixation with superficial adornment. Venus is an energy that can raise us to the highest or trap us in the lowest.

Along with Mercury, Venus is always near the Sun; she never gets more than around two signs away, and moves back and forth on either side of the Sun. Consider the quote from Emperor Julian that begins this chapter. There is a link in meaning between Venus and Sun - the Sun as giving light, Venus as disseminating the light, reflecting the light, perhaps harmonizing the light. The Sun is source of life and light, and Venus connects us to that source. Venus shapes and presents the light, diffusing, harmonizing, making temperate and beautiful. Making temperate is a very Venusian sort of concept, as it balances, harmonizes, puts in good proportion.

Sun - Source Texts

The Sun - Valens

In a nativity the all-seeing sun, nature's fire and intellectual light, the organ of mental perception, indicates kingship, rule, intellect, intelligence, beauty, motion, loftiness of fortune, the ordinance of the gods, judgment, public reputation, action, authority over the masses, the father, the master, friendship, noble personages, honors consisting of pictures, statues, and garlands, high priesthoods, <rule over> one's country <and over> other places.

Of the parts of the body, the sun rules the head; of the sense organs, it rules the right eye; of the trunk, it rules the heart; of the spiritual (i.e. the perceptive) faculties, the nerves.

Of materials, it rules gold; of fruits, it rules wheat and barley. It is of the day sect, yellowish, bitter in taste.

[COMMENT] The Sun is tied to perception and intellect. The Sun is light, and light is what you see by. Light is also connected to understanding and thinking, the way we speak of shedding light on something.

The Sun overall is related to honor, rulership, reputation, public standing, ranking in society and government. Sun and Jupiter have some similarities here.

There is no mention of the Sun as your identity, your self, as in modern Sun centered astrology.

Sun and Other Planets

Saturn and the Sun are at odds, giving and taking away possessions and friendships maliciously. Therefore those born under such a juncture suffer secret enmities and threats from great persons and are plotted against by some and live hated to the end. Playing their part well, they outlive most <of their enemies>. They are, however, not without resources, but are disturbed and long-suffering. They are self-controlled in this onslaught of reversals.

[COMMENT] Sun and Saturn are opposites in many ways. They rule opposite signs, rule light and darkness, warmth and cold, life and death. Saturn threatens and takes away everything the Sun bestows. In a good way, Saturn adds duration and age, so you see references to outliving enemies, being long-suffering, patient and self controlled. Saturn and Sun gives problems and reversals, but also gives the patience and endurance to deal with them

When **Jupiter and the Sun** are together, they produce noble and distinguished men, rulers, governors, dictators, vigorous men, honored and blessed by the crowd. These men are wealthy, rich, living with much spectacle. Sometimes however they are involved in uncertainties and hostility. Especially if the star <Jupiter> is found to be setting, they resort to greater showiness and make a pretense of the truth.

[COMMENT] Jupiter and Sun are very similar, so they complement and magnify each other here. In a good way it magnifies wealth, honor and fame. Unbalanced, it can be showiness, pretense, arrogance, where the grand display is superficial and false.

Venus and the Sun are in harmony, glorious, bestowers of good. They cause the association of male and female, they bring gifts and conveyances, and make men successful in their enterprises. Occasionally they make those men who take on popular leadership or trusts, those who are in charge of foreign/secure places, those thought worthy of stipends. These men, however, are not without grief with respect to wife and children, especially if Venus is setting.

[COMMENT] Venus brings out a lot of the best of the Sun, a magnanimous side. Sun and Venus are mentioned together as man and woman coming together, more so than Venus and Mars. The problems mentioned are Venusian and related to wife and children.

Mercury and the Sun make adaptable men with many friends, those flexible and self-controlled men who spend their careers in public places. These stars make pure, sensible men, men of good judgment, lovers of beauty, learned men, initiates into divine matters, beneficent, fond of their associates, independent, braggarts. These men endure reversals nobly, but are ineffective, suffering ups and downs in their livelihoods, experiencing vicissitudes. They are not poverty-stricken, but find a success proportional to the basis of their nativities.

[COMMENT] Both Sun and Mercury are related to understanding and wisdom, so that is amplified here when they are together. The Sun adds the element of fame, the public, recognition. The mention of reversals, ups and downs, comes from the instability of Mercury, and a lot of this description is mirrored in Mercury descriptions by itself.

The **Sun and the Moon** are good. They are productive of associations with the great and of high rank, as well as possession of estates, property, money, and adornment. These stars cause men to be successful in business enterprises and to receive profit. If the basis <of the nativity> is found to be great, men become leaders of cities, in charge of affairs, preeminent among the masses, gifted with a very high public image, munificent, governing, ruling, unsurpassed, and possessing a kingly property and spirit. Those starting with a moderate/ average fortune become lucky and are called blessed. The good, however, does not last for this type of person, because of the waning configuration of the Moon.

[COMMENT] Both Sun and Moon can relate to success, abundance and profit. Sun is leader of cities, Moon is the masses who are led, as the Sun shines on the Moon who reflects his light back. Note the instability here comes from the Moon in its phases, its waxing and waning.

Sun - Abu Mashar

14 As for the Sun, his nature is heating [and] drying.

15 And he indicates the animal soul, light and glowing, the intellect, knowledge, understanding, and the middle of the lifespan.

16 And he indicates kings, leaders, commanders, rulership, nobility, crowds of people, power, a struggle to overcome, fame, brilliance, arrogance, an overbearing attitude, vanity, self-importance, a good reputation, a desire for leadership and assets, and a powerful love of gold.

17 And he indicates an abundance of speech, a love of cleanliness, and treats badly those who meet with him and get close to him with extreme insult, and the people most on the brink of that are those closest to him by place, while the most fortunate of them are those far from him; one who assembles with him will not have renown, nor will any vestige of him be seen: he will be put aright and corrupted, benefited and harmed, be fortunate and made unfortunate, raised up at one time and falling at another.

18 And he indicates the matter of religion and the hereafter, judges, sages, fathers, middle brothers, the multitude, and pure clarity in which there is nothing, and [such a man] mixes with the people, yielding to them [and] granting whatever things are asked about, having power over evildoers and the lords of disobedience.

[COMMENT] Notice verse 17, how those close to the Sun are treated badly and insulted, those far away are treated better. That is about the Sun and combustion - people too close to the Sun get burnt. The Sun is much more benefic when you are far enough from the rays that they are moderated somewhat.

Sun is the middle lifespan, the early mature years, since it is the middle of the seven planets in the Chaldean order.

Here Sun shares some of the connections with religion that we see in Jupiter, and shares the emphasis on knowledge with Mercury. With Mercury it is knowledge from an active, rapidly moving mind, a kind of commerce of ideas. With Sun it is knowledge as light, clarity, understanding. The metaphor is different so the meaning is a bit different.

The Sun - Al-Biruni

NATURES OF THE PLANETS

Sun is hot and dry, the heat predominant. Maleficent when near, beneficent at a distance. Male. Diurnal. Penetrating. Pungent, shining reddish-yellow, its colour is said to be that of the lord of the hour. Most expert, noble, well-known and generous things.

BUILDINGS

King's and Sultan's palaces.

RELATIONS AND CONNECTIONS, FIGURE AND FACE

Fathers and brothers, slaves. Large head, complexion white inclining to yellow, long hair, yellow in the white of the eye, stammers, large paunch with folds.

DISPOSITION AND MANNERS

Intelligent and knowledgeful, patient, chaste, but sensual, eager for knowledge, power and victory, seeking a good name for helping others, friendly, hot-tempered but quickly recovering repose.

ACTIVITIES, INSTINCTS AND MORALS

Longing for power and government, hankering after wealth and management of worldly affairs, and imposing will on the ignorant, reproving evil-doers, harsh with opponents. If Sun is in exaltation the position is favorable to kings, if in fall to those in rebellion.

CLASSES OF PEOPLE

Kings, nobles, chiefs, generals, officials, magistrates, physicians, societies.

RELIGIONS, PICTURES OF PLANETS

Wearing a crown; Magians, Mithraists. A man seated on something like a shield on wheels drawn by four oxen, in his right a staff on which he rests, in his left a mace gurz, beads; another picture: man seated, face like a circle, holding reins of four horses.

TRADES AND PROFESSION

Receiving, giving and selling gold brocades.

The Sun - William Ramesey

[TEXT] We are by God's blessing come now to the Sun,... placed in the midst of all the Planets, being the chief light and president of them all, sitting as a Judge or King among his nobles; For as Saturn, Jupiter and Mars are placed above his sphere, so are Venus, Mercury and Luna beneath him; wherefore some of the Ancients have ascribed to him chief rule, and made him, as it were, an Emperor among the Stars.

Saturn is his Vice-roy, for that all Planets give unto him their light, or do homage and reverence unto him, by reason of his slowness.

[NOTE] Since Saturn is the slowest moving planets, all other planets make aspects by applying to Saturn, and that is what Ramesey is talking about here.

[TEXT] Jupiter hath assigned him chief rule and dominion in the Realm, for that he is of a temperate, sober, good, honest and religious inclination.

Mars is his chief Captain, or General of all his Forces.

Venus is Receiver, or Master-Comptroller of his House, by reason she is nearer Sol than any other.

Mercury hath assigned him chief Secretary of State, by reason when the King goeth any Progress or Journey, he goeth, and when the King stayeth, so doth also Mercury, for he is never far from his beck.

Luna is his Standard-bearer, being furthest from him; she is also, as I may say, Ambassador, Messenger &c. to do his business.

The fixed Stars of several magnitudes are Officers and Commanders under these; I mean those especially of the first, second and third magnitude; the other are only subjects, as it were, to the above named, or equivalent to common people.

104

Wherefore then upon the meetings of these Superiors, are concluded the rise, subversion, confirmation, alteration, prosperity, scarcity, plenty, poverty, beginning and subversion of States, Kingdoms, Empires, Common-wealths and what not? nay and the whole government of the Elements and this Elementary world, and all things and causes external and internal in them, as in a Council or Senate, &c.

When his is well dignified, the King and Nobles shall exceed and increase in glory and renown; Corn, Beasts and Birds shall be plentiful; the people generally prosperous and successful, and all things in good condition, whereof the Sun hath any signification: All this is meant, if he be Lord of the year in any annual Revolution; but if he be weak, judge the contrary.

Quality of men when well placed - Emperors, Kings, Monarchs, Princes, Dukes, Marquesses, and indeed all Noble and High-born people, and in general all Gentlemen, and those that are in office or command of superiority in City, Town or Country; Coiners, Masters of the Mint, Goldsmiths, Spinners of Gold and Silver, and all such neat Trades, Silver and the like.

When ill placed - Tyrants, Usurpers, Constables, Head-boroughs, and all such as bear any petty or usurped authority.

He is author of magnanimity, state and majesty, heat, &c.

Of Herbs, Saffron, Mary-gold, Balm, Ginger, Sallendine Vervine, which being gathered under its proper constellation, driveth away evil Spirits; and it is also used in prophesying; Ambery, Rosemary, Musk, Cinnamon, Lignum Aloes, Barley, Lavender, Sweet Marjoram, Pepper, Frankincense, Honey, Aromaticus, &c.

Of Trees, the Bay-tree, the Ash, Cedar, Ivy, the Vine, the Orange and Lemon tree.

Of Birds, the Phoenix, Swan, Cock, Hawk, Nightingale, Lark, the Buzzard &c.

Of Stones, Aetites, the stone called the eye of the Sun, because it is like the apple of the eye in forms, the Carbuncle, the Chrysolate, the stone called Iris, the stone Heliotropion, the Hyacinth, the stone Pyrophylus, the stone Pantaurus, Pantherus or Pantochras, in the Scripture it is called Evanthum; the Topaz, Ruby, Diamond.

The learned and most famous Cornelius Agrippa, Lib 1. Chap. 23 of his Occulta Philosophia saith, that Albertus Magnus and William of Paris gave to these stone these virtues as followeth.

Aetites, or the stone that is found in the Eagle's Nest, cureth the Falling-sickness, and poisons.

The eye of the Sun, is singular good for comforting the brain, and strengthening the eye-sight.

The Carbuncle, is of great virtue against airy and vaporous poison.

The Chrysolite, is of marvellous operation, in preserving the Lungs, and helpeth much those that are Asthmatical; and if it be bored through and filled with the Mane of an Ass, and bound to the left arm, it driveth away idle imaginations, melancholy fears and foolishness.

The Iris, it is like the Crystal in color, it commonly having six Corners; it being part held in the shadow and part in the rays or beams of the Sun, it gathereth the rays of the Sun unto itself, and reflecteth them again in the form of a Rainbow.

The Heliotropion, is in color green like a Jasper, speckled with red; this causeth the bearer to be constant, renowned, famous, and conduceth to long life; it is said to turn the beams of the Sun into the color of blood, viz., when it is joined to the juice of the herb of the same name and put into water, it dazzleth the sight so much that the bearer can hardly see it by the help of the aforesaid herb.

The Hyacinth, is good against poison and pestiferous vapors; it keepeth the bearer safe and acceptable; it conduceth also to riches and wit; it strengthens the heart, being held in the mouth, and wonderfully cheereth the mind.

The Pyrophilus as Aesculapius maketh mention, there is a certain poison for very cold, which preserves the heart of man (being taken out) from burning, so that if for any time it be put into the fire, it is turned into a stone; whenced it is called Pyrophilus from the fire. It is marvelously efficacious against poison, and it makes the bearer renowned and dreadful to his enemies.

The Pantaura is of that sympathetical virtue that it draweth other stones to it as a lode-stone doth iron; admirable against poisons.

[NOTE] The section on the virtues of stones appears only in the chapter on the Sun, and there are no corresponding sections in the chapters for the other planets. I am including it here to give an idea of the kinds of powers associated with the Sun.

[TEXT] Of Metals or Minerals, the Sun ruleth Gold.

Of Fishes, the Sea-Calf, whose Nature is to resist lightning, Shell-fish, the Star-fish for her parching heat, and the fishes called Strombi that follow their King, and Margari which have a King also; these Margari being dried, are fixed into a stone of a golden color, as witnesseth Cornelius Agrippa.

Of Beasts, all such Beasts as are stately, furious, bold, strong and invincible, as the Lion, Crocodile, Wolf, Ram, Boar, Bull, Horse, and Baboon, of the which it is recorded, that he barketh every hour in the day, viz. twelve times in a day, and that in the Equinoctial times of the year he pisseth twelve times, viz, every hour, also as often in the night.

Moreover the Aegyptians did use to preserve them amongst their hallowed things; for that by them they knew the time of the Conjunction of Sol and Luna, for after the aforesaid Conjunction, the male Baboon will neither look up nor eat, but goes still dejected, as it were lamenting the ravishment of the Moon, with this disdainful passion; in like manner the Female at that time sendeth forth blood out of her womb of Conception; for which cause the Egyptians signify by a Baboon the Moon, and her rising by his standing upright, holding his hands up toward heaven.

Of Places, Prince's Palaces, Courts, Houses, all magnificent Buildings, Halls, Dining-rooms, Parlors &c.

In journeys he giveth good success.

He signifieth hot and dry Diseases, palpitation of the heart, infirmities of the eyes, cramps, soundings, giddiness in the head, diseases and infirmities of the mouth and brain, Catarrhs, rotten Fevers, &c.

The Sun - William Lilly

[SOL.] The Sun is placed in the middle of all Planets, and is called amongst the Ancients, both Poets and Historians, Sol, Titan, Ilioa, Phebus, Apollo, Pean, Osyris, Diespiter: It's needless to mention his Colour, being so continually visible to all mortal men: He passeth through all the twelve Signs of the Zodiac in one year, or 365 days and certain hours:

[MOTION.] His mean motion is 59 min 8 seconds, yet his diurnal motion is sometimes 57m 16 seconds, sometimes more, never exceeding 61 minutes and six seconds. He always moves in the Ecliptic, and is ever void of latitude, so that it is very improper in any Astrologian to speak of the Sun his latitude.

[HOUSE.] He hath only the Sign of Leo for his House, and Aquarius for his Detriment. He is Exalted in the 19 degree of Aries, and receives his Fall in 19 Libra.

The Sun is always direct, and never can be said to be Retrograde, it's true, he moveth more slowly at one time then another.

[NATURE.] He is naturally Hot, Dry, but more temperate then Mars; is a Masculine, Diurnal Planet, Equivalent if well dignified to a Fortune.

[MANNERS WHEN WELL DIGNIFIED.] Very faithful, keeping their promises with all punctuality, a kind of itching desire to Rule and Sway where he comes: Prudent, and of incomparable Judgment; of great Majesty and Stateliness, Industrious to acquire Honour and a large Patrimony, yet as willingly departing therewith again; the Solar man usually speaks deliberately, but not many words, and those with great confidence and command of his own affection; full of Thought, Secret, Trusty, speaks deliberately, and notwithstanding his great Heart, yet is he Affable, Tractable, and very humane to all people, one loving

Sumptuousness and Magnificence, and whatever is honourable; no sordid thoughts can enter his heart, &c.

[WHEN ILL DIGNIFIED.] Then the Solar man is Arrogant and Proud, disdaining all men, cracking of his Pedigree, he is Pur-blind in Sight and Judgment, restless, troublesome, domineering; a mere vapour, expensive, foolish, endued with no gravity in words, or soberness in Actions, a Spend-thrift, wasting his Patrimony, and hanging after an other men's charity, yet thinks all men are bound to him, because a Gentleman born.

[CORPORATURE.] Usually the Sun presents a man of a good, large and strong Corporature, a yellow, saffron Complexion, a round, large Forehead: goggle Eyes or large, sharp and piercing; a Body strong and well composed, not so beautiful as lovely, full of health, their hair yellowish, and thereof quickly bald, much Hair on their Beard, and usually an high ruddy Complexion, and their bodies fleshy, in conditions they are very bountiful honest, sincere, well-minded, of great and large Heart, High-minded, of healthful Constitution, very humane; yet sufficiently Spirited, not Loquacious.

In the Sun, we can only say he is Oriental in the Figure, or in the Oriental quarter of the Figure, or Occidental, &c. all other Planets are either Oriental, when they rule, appear before him in the morning. Occidental, when they are seen above the Earth after he is set.

[QUALITY OF MEN AND THEIR PROFESSIONS.] He signifieth Kings, Princes, Emperors, &c. Dukes, Marquesses, Earls, Barons, Lieutenants, Deputy-Lieutenants of Countries, Magistrates, Gentlemen in general, Courtiers, desirers of Honour and Preferment, Justices of Peace, Majors, High-Sheriffs, High-Constables, great Huntsmen, Lieutenants, Deputy-Lieutenants, Stewards of Noblemen's houses, the principal Magistrate of any City, Town, Castle or Country-Village, yea, though a petty Constable, where no better, or greater Officer is; Goldsmiths, Brasiers, Pewterers, Coppersmiths, Minters of Money.

[SICKNESS.] Pimples in the Face, Palpitation or Trembling, or any Diseases of the Brain or Heart, Timpanies, Infirmities of the Eyes, Cramps, sudden swoonings, Diseases of the Mouth, and sunking Breaths, Catarrhs, rotten Fevers; principally in man he governeth the Heart, the Brain and right Eye, and vital Spirit, in Women the left Eye.

[COLOURS AND SAVORS.] Of Colors he ruleth the Yellow, the colour of Gold, the Scarlet or the deer Red, some say Purple: In Savors, he liketh well a mixture of Sour and Sweet together, or Aromatical flavor, being a little Bitter and Stiptical, but withal Confortative and a little sharp.

[HERBS AND PLANTS.] Those Plants which are subject to the Sun do smell pleasantly, are of good flavor, their Flowers are yellow or reddish, are in growth of Majestical form, they love open and Sunshine places, their principal Virtue is to strengthen the Heart, and comfort the Vitals, to clear the Eye-sight, resist Poison, or to dissolve any Witchery, or Malignant Planetary Influences; and they are Saffron, the Laurel, the Pomecitron, the Vine, Enula Campana, Saint johns-wort, Amber, Musk, Ginger, Herb grace, Balm, Marigold, Rosemary, Rosafolis, Cinnamon, Celendine, Eye-bright, Peony, Barley, Cinquefoile, Spikenard, Lignum Aloes, Arsenic.

[TREES.] Ash-tree, Palm, Laurel-tree, the Myrrh-tree, Frankincense, the Cane-tree or Planet, the Cedar, Heletrepion, the Orange and Lemon-tree.

[BEASTS.] The Lion, the Horse, the Ram, the Crocodile, the Bull, Goat, Night-worms or Glow-worms. [COMMENT - I wonder if glow-worms are solar because they give light.]

[FISHES.] The Sea-Calf or Sea-Fox, the Crabfish, the Starfish.

[BIRDS.] The Eagle, the Cock, the Phoenix, Nightingale, Peacock, the Swan, the Buzzard, the Slye Cantharis, the Goshawk.

[PLACES.] Houses, Courts of Princes, Palaces, Theatres, all magnificent Structures being clear and decent, Halls, Dining Rooms.

[MINERALS OR METALS.] Amongst the Elements Sun hath domination of fire and clear shining flames, over metals, he ruleth Gold.

[STONES.) The Hyacinth, Chrysolite, Adamant, Carbuncle, the Etites stone found in Eagle's nests, the Pantaure, if such a stone be the Ruby.

[WEATHER.] He produceth weather according to the season; in the spring gentle moisting Showers; in the Summer heat in extremity if with Mars; in Autumn mists; in Winter small Rain.

[WINDS.] He loves the East part of the World; and that wind which proceeds from that quarter.

[ORB.] Is 15. degrees before any aspect; and so many after separation.

[ANGEL.] Michael.

[DAY OF THE WEEK.] He ruleth Sunday the first hour thereof, and the eight; and in numbers the first and fourth; and in conceptions the fourth month. His friends are all the Planets except Saturn, who is his Enemy.

The Sun - General Notes

"If the Sun is beyond a visible essence, it will have a supermundane nature. For the world is visible and tangible, and has a body. Hence, we must survey the Sun in a twofold respect; viz. as one of the seven planets, and as a leader of wholes; as mundane and supermundane, according to the latter of which he emits a splendidly divine light... And if beginning from visible natures, you are willing to speak of such as are invisible, the light of the Sun gives splendour to the whole world, causes a corporeal-formed nature to be divine, and wholly filled through the whole of itself with life. But it leads souls through undefiled light, imparts to them a pure and elevating power, and governs the world by its rays. And it likewise fills souls with empyrean fruits."

- Proclus, On the Theology of Plato
  translated by Thomas Taylor

Notice that there is nothing here about the Sun standing for you, the person. That use of the Sun likely traces back to the Theosophist Alan Leo, who started what we think of as Sun sign astrology around the beginning of the twentieth century. In traditional astrology you look to the rising sign and its ruler, and to planets in the first house, to represent the person.

The Sun has less to do with identity and more with glory, honor and power. In traditional astrology the Sun has much more to do with public standing and reputation than it does with identity. The Sun overall is related to honor, rulership, reputation, public standing, ranking in society and government. Sun and Jupiter have some similarities here, as do Sun and Mercury. Traditional astrology is not centered on the individual human and their welfare; it is centered on the society, the cosmos. Cosmos is from a Greek word meaning something like city or political unit, and it has the same connotation as our modern word cosmopolitan. A person's natal chart has much more do with how the person will fit in the overall order. Individual identity is much less heavily emphasized. The universe in traditional astrology does not revolve around the individual; it revolves around the King who is the center of the collective whole. Recall the section from William Ramesey where he speaks of the Sun as Emperor, and then assigns each of the other planets a role within the King's realm.

No other planet comes anywhere near overshadowing the Sun, so the Sun owns reputation, glory and power. There is considerable overlap between the meanings of the Sun and Jupiter, since both have to do with rulership, with royalty, with giving life in a benevolent way.

The Sun in its daily and yearly movement defines the measure of time for us; the measure of day and year would have no meaning without the Sun. Because of that the Sun is also related to overall measure and structure, and to cycles of time.

Like the other light, the Moon, the Sun can be either benefic or malefic according to its overall condition. The Sun when benefic is the source of warmth, light and life, and makes things grow. The Sun malefic can burn, scorch, destroy, cause fires and droughts.

The Sun also has a connection with perception and understanding. The Sun gives light, sheds light, and light has the connotations of understanding, of consciousness, and of divinity. There is quite a bit of overlap in meaning with Mercury in this area, and that makes sense when you consider that Mercury stays so very close to the Sun, and is continually crossing back and forth behind it.

Consider the quote from the Platonist writer Proclus at the start of this section. In the Platonic tradition each of the planets of astrology exist on multiple levels, and the physical planet is like the garment or vessel of a divine being, a god on a higher spiritual level. The planets are not just planets, they are divine expressions, and the gods work in our world. This means that, along with the physical attributions of the Sun, there is also a dimension of the Sun as an expression of divinity, as conveying spiritual light, life and wisdom. For the Platonists this is not a metaphor, it is an expression of a powerful spiritual reality.

In Platonic tradition the gods of the planets are at a high spiritual level characterized by unity, by a oneness with the One and the Good that is the underlying source of all. Because of this, any one of the gods can be the one god, the expression of the one. Any one of the gods can connect us to the highest divinity. While this is true of the gods in general, it is particularly applicable to the Sun as the source of light and life. In that sense, worshiping the Sun as the supreme God and Father of all is not simple idolatry, glorifying a physical body in the sky. The Sun in that sense is a window to the divine, so worshiping the Sun is a valid way to connect to worshiping the one source of all. I find that meditations on the Sun as an emblem of the One God can be very powerful and immediate.

We mentioned the affinity in meaning between Jupiter and the Sun, and that applies here. There is a sense in which Jupiter is the father and creator, and the Sun is an expression of the father. In another sense Jupiter is the father, the creator or architect, and the Sun is Son, the main expression, the embodiment or only-begotten Sun of the father.

Mars - Source Texts

Mars - Valens

[TEXT] Mars indicates force, wars, plunderings, screams, violence, whoring, the loss of property, banishment, exile, alienation from parents, capture, the deaths of wives, abortions, love affairs, marriages, the loss of goods, lies, vain hopes, strong-armed robbery, banditry, looting, quarrels among friends, anger, fighting, verbal abuse, hatreds, lawsuits.

Mars brings violent murders, slashings and bloodshed, attacks of fever, ulceration, boils, burns, chains, torture, masculinity, false oaths, wandering, embassies under difficult circumstances, actions involving fire or iron, craftwork, masonry. In addition Mars causes commands, campaigns and leadership, infantrymen, governorships, hunting, wild game, falls from heights or from animals, weak vision, strokes.

Of the body parts, Mars rules the head, the seat, the genitals; of the internal parts, it rules the blood, the sperm ducts, the bile, the elimination of excrement, the parts in the rear, the back, and the underside. It controls the hard and the abrupt. Of materials, it rules iron, decoration of clothing (because of Aries), as well as wine and beans. It is of the night sect, red in color and acid in taste.

[COMMENT] This is mostly very violent and negative - most of the connotations have to do with violence and its effects. Notice the phrase, 'It rules the hard and the abrupt.' Those qualities run through most of the attributions. Mars being hot and dry runs as a theme through most of this section. The actions described are quick, abrupt, violent, hot, or working with heat. This can be war, it can also be hunting. Verbally, hot and dry mars attacks with words, so you have anger, quarreling, hatred, lawsuits and such. It also includes violent or negative intent, so torture is mentioned. The positive qualities mentioned are related to war and violence, the positive qualities an effective soldier would need.

The diseases mentioned either have to do with heat or inflammation, like ulcers and boils, or they are conditions that come on quickly and strike you down like strokes. Iron and craftwork is working with a metal using fire, and is specifically associated with iron.

There is a mention of love affairs, and marriages, but this is a minor theme. You do not see the pairing of Mars and Venus as male and female sexuality that you find in modern texts.

Mars with Other Planets

[TEXT] **Saturn and Mars** are hostile, productive of reversals and ruin. They bring family quarrels, disharmony, and hatred, along with treachery, plots, malevolence, and trials. However, if these stars are not[?] in their own or in operative signs, and if they have benefics in aspect, they produce distinguished and noble nativities, although unsteady in their happiness and prone to unexpected dangers and treachery.

[COMMENT] Mars and Saturn are opposites and both are malefic, so the combination is predictably violent and destructive. On the positive side, if Saturn and Mars are well dignified - I suspect the sentence should read, 'are in their own signs', rather than 'are not', which is why I added the question mark - then the distinguished and noble nativities could relate to respect or honor, but coming from power and force rather than cooperation. Even the reference to noble nativities talks about dangers and treachery - it might be respect, but it is based on power, mutual hostility and distrust.

[TEXT] **Jupiter and Mars** make glorious and showy characters, friends of the great or of kings, distinguished governors and receivers of stipends, those making a career in public affairs or in campaigns, and those considered worthy of honor and status, but uncertain in their livelihoods and habits, tossing away their possessions.

[COMMENT] Combine Jupiter and Mars and you have people who are powerful, respected, but also likely feared. The high honor comes from Jupiter, the uncertainty and instability from Mars. By 'campaigns' I am pretty sure he means military campaigns.

[TEXT] **Venus and Mars** are at odds. They make men unsteady and weak of mind; they cause rivalry and murder; they cause men to have many friends, but to be blameworthy, shameless, fickle, and equally prone to intercourse with men or women; to be malicious, and plotters of murder by poison. These stars cause men to remain with neither the good nor the bad, to be slandered and reviled because of their friendships, to be spendthrift, flitting from one occupation to another, to be eager for many things, to be wronged by women and because of them to suffer crises, upsets, and debts.

[COMMENT] The main thing to notice is that sexual attraction and activity is a theme here, but not the major theme by any means. Traditionally sex is mostly attributed to Venus, and very little to Mars. Here the references to sex imply an out of control lust. This paragraph mostly combines the rashness of Mars with the weakness of Venus. The combination is unsteady and unreliable.

[TEXT] **Mercury and Mars** are not good. They cause hostility, lawsuits, reversals, malice, betrayals, wrongs from superiors or inferiors. These stars make some men athletic, martial, commanding, beneficent, inquisitive <of the occult>, getting a livelihood in a varied manner. They resort to forgery in order to embezzle, steal, and loot, and having fallen into debt and expenses, they bring on themselves infamy and hot pursuit. If the configuration is afflicted, men meet with accusations and imprisonment, and they suffer loss or confiscation of goods.

[COMMENT] Both Mars and Mercury by themselves are fast moving, unsteady, sometimes untrustworthy and hostile, so the combination is mostly negative. Combine Mars as violent plus Mercury as money and commerce, and you get stealing, embezzling and so on.

Final note - in the Valens text that I have, in the section on the combinations of two planets, there is no text on the combination of Mars and the Moon.

Mars - Abu Mashar

11 As for Mars, his nature is heating, drying, fiery, yellow bile, and its taste bitter.

[Note: In the original, the following verse 12 is a single sentence which is a long list of widely varied items separated by commas; I find it to be very dense and hard to read on the page. Here I break it up into smaller clauses to make it easier to scan. The words in brackets in this section were added by the translator.]

12 And he indicates youth, strength, mental sharpness, heat, fires, conflagration, every matter occurring suddenly,

a king who has power and valor, cavalrymen, chief commanders, soldiers, the companions of the Sultan,

oppression, coercion, war, killing, fighting, courage, hardiness, seeking glory, renown, and rank;

the instruments of war, those entrusted with mobilizing wars, seeking retaliation, provoking discord, those craving groups and splitting apart, warring with one another,

becoming a thief, digging, stealing, highway robbery, haughtiness, risk-taking, anger,

regarding forbidden things as permissible,

punishment, fetters, beating, imprisonment, restriction,

running away, desertion, capture, prisoners,

fear, conflict, injustice, anger, fury, recklessness, harshness, a coarseness of heart, foolishness, stubbornness, with scarce examination, haste, quickness in things, daring, bad in expression, ugliness of speech (and its coarseness and harshness), indecency of the tongue,

revealing love and affection, glad tidings, extravagance in speech, [using] wiles in answering quickly [but with] repentance in it [afterwards],

a scarcity of piety and scarcity of fidelity but an abundance of lying, slander, and debauchery; swearing false oaths, deception, cunning, bad works, a scarcity of good, the undermining of suitable things,

an abundance of thought in matters, whims, independence of opinion from situation to situation but quickly going back,

an insolent look, little shame, an abundance of trouble and exertion, travels, exile, isolation, being a bad neighbor,

fornication, ugly sexual intercourse,

jokes, liveliness,

the movement which happens at the time of a woman giving birth, the labor pains of a pregnant woman, the death of women in pregnancy, the cutting of a child in the womb, and the miscarriage of a fetus.

13 And he indicates middle brothers, the management of riding animals, veterinary science, the protection of sheep, the treatment of wounds, the craft of iron and working with it, the circumcision of boys, the desecration of tombs, and the robbing of the dead.

[COMMENT]

Abu Mashar's text is recognizably continuing the same themes we saw in Valens. Mars is hot, dry, sharp, abrupt, violent. Yellow bile is a body humor that corresponds to the choleric or fiery temperament. Mars is related to anything to do with war, violence and discord, physical or verbal. As character Mars has fiery and violent qualities like anger, fury, recklessness, rebellion, stubbornness and so on. Mars does not take orders from others very well, although that is somewhat offset by the loyalty you would to a leader in charge of an army. Take the fiery and reckless quality and apply it to speech and you get crude speech, indecency, coarseness, lack of shame.

Mars is associated with youth, especially young men involved in military and competitive activities. Mars also relates to the risk-taking and seeking glory that goes with ambitious youth.

Mars is also somewhat of a loner planet - people standing over against each other - and with its malefic side it associates with thieves, robbery and so on. We also find the theme of Mars being unstable, fast moving, shifting. The planet is not reliable and it doesn't stay put, so it also has a connection with moving around a lot or being fast moving.

In modern astrology we often associate Mars and Venus together with sexual activity, but traditionally sex by itself is largely Venusian, and Mars adds a crude, obscene and sometimes violent element to sex.

Concerning childbirth Mars relates to sharp events right at the moment of birth, like the labor pains, or cutting a child out - birth by C-section would be very Martial - and also the hazards of birth including pain and death of the mother.

Mars - Al-Biruni

NATURES OF THE PLANETS

Mars is extremely hot and dry. The lesser malefic. Male (some say female). Nocturnal. Bitter. Dark red. Hot, hard, sharp and red things. Length, dryness and coarseness. Waste, hard and stony land.

[COMMENT] All of this aligns with main themes we have seen. Land that is hot and dry would be a stony wasteland. This is the only instance I am aware of where Mars is said to possibly be female.

BUILDINGS

Fire-temples, fireplaces and firewood, roadside fires and the vessels necessary for the art of the potter.

RELATIONS AND CONNECTIONS, FIGURE AND FACE

Brothers of middle age. Tall large head, small eyes and ears and fine forehead, sharp grey eyes, good nose, thin lips, lank hair, reddish, long fingers, long steps.

[COMMENT] Mars is very commonly associated with brothers. Being a middle planet in terms of distance from the earth, it is associated with middle age.

DISPOSITION AND MANNERS

Confused opinions, ignorant, rash and evil conduct, licentious, bold quarrelsome, unsteady, untrustworthy, violent, shameless, unchaste but quickly repentant, a deceiver, cheerful, bright, friendly and pleasant faced.

123

[COMMENT] Hot, abrupt, thoughtless action. It has a rebellious streak so it is not reliable or trustworthy.

ACTIVITIES, INSTINCTS AND MORALS

Marriage, traveling, litigation, business going to ruin, false testimony, lustful, a bad companion, solitary, spiteful and tricky.

CLASSES OF PEOPLE

Leaders, cavalry, troops, opponents, disputants in assembly.

RELIGIONS, PICTURES OF PLANETS

Idolaters, wine-bibbers, dressed in red. Young man seated on two lions, in the right hand a drawn sword in the left a battle-axe; another picture: mounted on a bay horse, helmet on head, in the left hand a spear adorned with red roses, pennon flag, in the right hand head of a man, clad in red.

TRADES AND PROFESSIONS

Lawmaking, selling and making armour, blacksmiths craft, grooms, shepherd, butchers, veterinary surgeons, surgeons, circumcisers, sellers of hounds, sickles, copper, beer, brigandage, contention, housebreaking, highwaymen, grave-robbers and prison, torture, execution.

[COMMENT] Some of these trades relate to war, and some of them relate to sharp cutting instruments - blacksmith is a particularly Martial trade as it uses fire to shape iron into cutting implements, and tools of surgery and of war. Mars then would also relate to trades involving cutting or trimming. Some of these are also rebellious, violent, painful, dangerous.

Mars - William Ramesey

When he is Lord of the Year, strong and well placed, all such as belong to arms, as soldiers, and the like, shall be fortunate and in good condition, and shall overcome their enemies; there shall be also, during that Revolution, sufficient and plenty of rain, and at such times (and no other) as convenient and requisite; and the people shall be prosperous and happy; but if he be weak, judge the contrary.

He is the author of anger, haste, choler, and ruleth these dispositions in man; hot, fiery and dry.

When well placed, Conquerors, Usurpers, Tyrants, Generals of Armies, and all Soldiers in general, Physicians, Apothecaries, Chirurgions [Surgeons], Alchemists, Marshalls, Butchers, Gunners, Watch-makers, Barbers, Armourers, and all such as use Iron tools, Curriers, Tanners, Gamesters, Dyers, Carpenters, Cooks, Cutlers, Tailors, Smiths, Bankers.

When he is ill placed and not strong, he denotes hangmen, thieves, bailiffs, sergeants, cutters by the high-way, murderers, jailors, and all cut-throat people.

He is author of passion, extravagancy, heat and choler.

Savors, Sharp, bitter, and unpleasant.

Herbs, all such herbs as are hot and dry, and such as have sharp-pointed leaves, and are red, and usually grow on dry places and such as are barren and hard stony places; the thistle, Devils-milk, brambles, briers, nettles, onions, radish, mustard-seed, ginger, pepper, garlic, hemlock, tamarind, horehound, leeks.

All trees that are thorny or prickly.

Birds, The Hawk, Kite, Raven, Vulture, Owl, Crow, Magpie and all ravenous birds or birds of prey.

Stones, Blood-stone, Load-stone, Jasper, Adamant, the Amethyst of diverse colors.

Of Metals, Iron Steel, Arsenic, Antimony, Brimstone and red Vermilion.

Of fishes, the Shark, Pike, Barbel, Fork-fish, all stinging Water-Serpents, and hurtful Fish.

Of Beasts, the Mastiff, Wolf, Tiger, Cockatrice, Panther, and all such beasts as are ravenous and bold.

Of weather, Thunder, lightning, fiery-meteors, pestilential air, and in it strange apparitions, &c.

All places that are appertaining to fire and blood, as slaughter-houses, Furnaces, Smiths shops &c.

In journeys, he portends thieving, sacking, robbing, flaying, much danger or hurts, viz. to the Traveler, if Mars be Significator, and weak, and ill-placed &c.

Of Diseases, Fevers, and those burning, contagious and pestilential; Megrims [Migraines], overflowing of the Gall, Phrenzies, the Plague, distempers through the whole body, Shingles, Fistulaes, Stone in the reins [kidneys], yellow Jaundice, and all such diseases as proceed from excess of Choler, Passion and Anger; all diseases proceeding from the Gall, Putrefaction of blood, &c.

Mars - William Lilly

MARS doth in order succeed Jupiter, whom the Ancients sometimes called Mavors, Ares, Pyrois, Gradivus; he is less in body then Jupiter or Venus, and appeareth to our sight of a shining, fiery, sparkling colour, he finisheth his course in the Zodiac in one year 321 days, or thereabouts; his greatest latitude North is 4, 31 min. his South is 6 degr. and 47.

He hath Aries for his Day-house, and Scorpio for his Night-house; he is exalted in 28 degr. of Capricorn, and is depressed in 28 Cancer, he receiveth detriment in Libra and Taurus; he is retrograde 80 days; stationary before direction two days; after, but one day.

[NATURE.] He is Masculine, Nocturnal Planet, in nature hot and dry, choleric and fiery, the lesser Infortune, author of Quarrels, Strifes, Contentions.

[MANNERS WHEN WELL DIGNIFIED.] In feats of War and Courage invincible, scorning any should exceed him, subject to no Reason, Bold, Confident, Immovable, Contentious, challenging all Honour to themselves, Valiant, lovers of War and things pertaining thereunto, hazarding himself to all Perils, willingly will obey no body; nor submit to any, a large reporter of his own Acts, one that fights all things in comparison of Victory, and yet of prudent behavior in his own affairs.

[WHEN ILL PLACED.] Then he is Prattler without modesty or honesty, a lover of Slaughter and Quarrels, Murder, Thievery, a promoter of Sedition, Frays and Commotions; and Highway-Thief, as wavering as the Wind, a Traitor, of turbulent Spirit, Perjurer, Obscene, Rash, Inhumane, neither fearing God or caring for man, Unthankful, Treacherous, Oppressors, Ravenous, Cheater, Furious, Violent.

[CORPORATURE.] Generally Martialists have this form; they are but middle Stature, their Bodies strong, and their Bones big, rather lean

127

then fat; their Complexion of a brown, ruddy colour, or flaxen, and many times crisping or curling, sharp hazel Eyes, and they piercing, a bold confident countenance, and the man active and fearless.

[ORIENTAL.] When Mars is Oriental, he signifies Valiant men, some white mixed with the redness, a decent tallness of Body, hairy of his Body.

[OCCIDENTAL.] Very ruddy Complexion'd, but mean in Stature, little Head, a smooth Body, and not hairy; yellow Hair, stiff, the natural humours generally more dry.

[PRINCES.] Ruling by Tyranny and Oppression, or Tyrants, Usurpers, new Conquerors.

[QUALITIES OF MEN AND PROFESSION.] Generals of Armies, Colonels, Captains, or any Soldiers having command in Armies, all manner of Soldiers, Physicians, Apothecaries, Alchemists, Gunners, Butchers, Marshals, Sergeants, Bailiffs, Hang-men, Thieves, Smiths, Bakers, Armourers, Watch-makers, Butchers, Tailors, Cutlers of Swords and Knives, Barbers, Dyers, Cooks, Carpenters, Gamesters, Bear-wards, Tanners, Carriers.

[DISEASES.] The Gall, the left Ear, tertian Fevers, pestilent burning Fevers, Migraines in the Head, Carbuncles, the Plague and all Plague-sores, Burnings, Ring-worms, Blisters Phrensies, mad sudden distempers in the Head, Yellow-jaundices, Bloody-flux, Fistulaes, all Wounds and Diseases in mens Genitories, the Stone both in the Reins (kidney) and Bladder, Scars or small Pocks in the Face, all hurts by Iron, the Shingles, and such other Diseases as arise by abundance of too much Choler, Anger or Passion.

[COLOUR AND SAVORS.] He delighteth in Red colour, or yellow, fiery and shining like Saffron; and in those Savors which are bitter, sharp and burn the Tongue; of Humors, Choler.

[HERBS.] The Herbs which we attribute to Mars are such as come near to a redness, whose leaves are pointed and sharp, whose taste is caustic and burning, love to grow on dry places, are corrosive and penetrating the Flesh and Bones with a most subtle heat: They are as followeth. The Nettle, all manner of Thistles, Rest-harrow or Cammock, Devils-milk or Petty spurge, the white and red Brambles, the white called vulgarly by the Herbalists Ramme, Lingwort, Onion, Scommony, Garlick, Mustard-seed, Pepper, Ginger, Leeks, Ditander, Hore-hound, Hemlock, red Sanders, Tamarindes, all Herbs attracting or drawing choler by Sympathy, Radish, Castoreum, Arsolarr, Assarum, Carduus, Benedictus, Cantharides.

[TREES.] All Trees which are prickly, as the Thorn, Chestnut.

[BEASTS AND ANIMALS.] Panther, Tiger, Mastiff, Vulture, Fox; of living creatures, those that are Warlike, Ravenous and Bold, the Castor [Beaver], Horse, Mule, Ostrich, the Goat, the Wolf, the Leopard, the wild Asse, the Gnats, Flies, Lapwing, Cockatrice, the Griffon, Bear.

[FISHES.] The Pike, the Shark. the Barbel, the Fork-fish, all stinking Worms, Scorpions.

[BIRDS.] The Hawk, the Vulture, the Kite or Glead, (all ravenous Fowl) the Raven, Cormorant, the Owl, (some say the Eagle) the Crow, the Pye.

[PLACES.] Smiths, Shops, Furnaces, Slaughter-houses, places where Bricks or Charcoals are burned, or have been burned, Chimneys, Forges.

[MINERALS.] Iron, Antimony, Arsenic, Brimstone, Ochre.

[STONES.] Adamant, Lodestone, Blood-stone, Jasper, the many coloured Amethyst, the Touch-stone, red Lead or Vermilion.

[WEATHER] Red clouds, Thunder, Lightning, Fiery impressions, and pestilent Airs, which usually appear after a long time of dryness and fair Weather, by improper and unwholesome Mists.

[WINDS.] He stirreth up the Western Winds.

[ORB.] His Orb is only seven degrees before and after any of his aspects.

[YEARS.] In man he governeth the flourishing time of Youth, and from 41 to 56.

[DAY OF THE WEEK.] He governeth Tuesday, and therein the first hour and eighth from Sun rise, and in Conception the third month.

[ANGEL.] Samael. His friends are only Venus; Enemies all the other Planets.

[COMMENT] Notice that sexual attraction or activity is not mentioned anywhere in this entire section. Venus rules sexual attraction and activity of any kind, male or female.

Mars - General Notes

"The triad of celestial Gods immediately above the Sun consists of Mars, Jupiter and Saturn, of which the first is the source of division and motion, perpetually separates, nourishes and excites the contrarieties of the universe, that the world may exist perfect and entire from all its parts. He requires, however, the assistance of Venus that he may insert order and harmony into things contrary and discordant."

- Proclus, On the Theology of Plato
  Translated by Thomas Taylor

Compared to a complex planet like the Moon or Mercury, the meanings of Mars are pretty straight-forward, and group around just a few common themes. Mars is hot and dry. The color of the planet in the sky is red, which is probably part of where these associations came from. Being hot, dry and malefic, its action is abrupt and fast. Being both dry and malefic, its action sunders, separates, breaks apart.

Compared to the other malefic Saturn, Mars is acute and Saturn is chronic. Saturn destroys by blocking, freezing, slowly rotting. Mars destroys by sundering, separating or piercing like a sword, or by burning like a fire. Mars rules war, conflict, violence and rebellion of all kinds. Its negative sides are related to violence and destruction.

Mars is associated with the faculty of anger, and anger here has a wider connotation than our modern sense of the term. The faculty of anger was thought to reside in the heart, between the gut or lower emotions and appetites below, and the head or higher thoughts and guidance. The faculty of anger includes a sense of courage, the willingness to be able to stand up and fight for what is morally right.

The positive sides of Mars are the virtues of the warrior, the soldier. There is strength, bravery, the ability to act decisively. It can relate to ruling, but if so it is a ruling by force, by coercion, by strength. Lilly brings out more of the admirable side of Mars, and it relates to the faculty of anger in this wider sense - courage, fearlessness, willingness to fight without regard to personal consequences. This is a virtue which is useful within a specific area, that of the military, defending a city from hostile attackers. Mars by itself would be destructive, so in the quote from Proclus at the start of this section he talks of balancing the virtues of Mars with the harmonizing and healing virtues of Venus.

As we have repeatedly noted, unlike modern astrology, there is very little emphasis on Mars and sexuality, with men from Mars and women from Venus. Sexuality of any kind and of either sex is mostly under the domain of Venus in traditional astrology. When we do see associations of Mars and sexuality it usually has a negative, violent or out of control quality. Mars is a loner planet; there is very little that is sociable about its qualities, the exception being the loyalty of soldiers who fight together. Mars divides people rather than bringing them together.

Many of the qualities now associated with the outer planet Uranus would be better assigned traditionally to Mars. Mars can be the outcast, the rebel, the revolutionary, the pioneer, bringing abrupt change, shaking up the established order. Add in some of the qualities of Mercury and you have covered pretty much all of the meanings of Uranus.

Before I close I want to consider some of the implications of the quote from the Platonist Proclus at the head of this essay. Mars is responsible for dividing and separating, and it is a necessary part of our world order. Our world is based on polar opposites, and division is part of what is needed to keep everything in motion. Mars is part of that process, and sometimes it is violent and often painful.

Another thing we need to remember is that the traditional world assumed that the military, conflict and warfare were part of the world order. No society could exist without a strong military, and without men being willing to serve as the warriors. As part of that, some people were considered as born to be warriors, and a professional warrior class is part of the ideal civilization presented by Plato in the *Republic*. That is not a uniquely Western assumption; the great Hindu classic that inspired Mohandas Gandhi, the *Bhagavad-Gita*, is a dialog between the avatar Krishna, and Arjuna, who is of the kshatriya or warrior class. The entire dialog takes place in the middle of a battlefield right at the commencement of perhaps the most horrible and bloody war in the *Mahabharata*, the long epic which is the setting of the *Gita*. Arjuna was a professional warrior; that was his duty, and there is a frequent refrain in the *Gita* of a set of instructions from Krishna ending with the words, therefore fight, O Arjuna. The avatar Krishna isn't there to make peace, he is there to assist Arjuna to fight and win.

Two of the earliest classic texts in the Greek tradition are the epic poems by Homer, the *Iliad* and the *Odyssey*. Both are records of wars. The planet Mars and his often violent characteristics are not a temporary aberration; they are a basic part of our world order. That is well worth thinking about, long and hard.

Jupiter - Source Texts

Jupiter - Valens

Jupiter indicates childbearing, engendering, desire, loves, political ties, acquaintance, friendships with great men, prosperity, salaries, great gifts, an abundance of crops, justice, offices, officeholding, ranks, authority over temples, arbitrations, trusts, inheritance, brotherhood, fellowship, beneficence, the secure possession of goods, relief from troubles, release from bonds, freedom, deposits in trust, money, stewardships,

Of the external body parts it rules the thighs and the feet. (Consequently in the games Jupiter governs the race.) Of the internal parts it rules the sperm, the uterus, the liver, the parts of the right side.

Of materials, it rules tin. It is of the day sect. In color it is grey verging on white and is sweet in taste.

[COMMENT] There are a couple of main themes here. Jupiter is giving life. Jupiter is abundance of all good things, growth, expansion, good times. We also see elevation, high rank, honor, and the power that goes with high office. Along with good fortune, Jupiter relates to money and control over money; money plus good fortune gives gifts, relief from trouble.

With the mention of authority over temples, there is another theme that will become more prominent through the tradition, and that is the connection of Jupiter with religion. I think this ties together with several themes. It is related to authority. It is also related to themes of brotherhood and fellowship, as religion provides a cohesive structure that binds people together. Summing it up, Jupiter is related to that overall benevolent structure that gives shape and form and does bring us together.

Jupiter in Combination

When Saturn and Jupiter are together, they are in agreement with each other, and they bring about benefits from legacies and adoptions, and they cause men to be masters of property consisting of land, to be guardians, managers of others' property, stewards, and tax gatherers.

[COMMENT] The two largest and outermost planets together have power, hence mastery and control of property. The combination seems to be predominantly Jupiterian with no sign of Saturn's negative effect. Jupiter brings out the best of Saturn.

When Jupiter and the Sun are together, they produce noble and distinguished men, rulers, governors, dictators, vigorous men, honored and blessed by the crowd. These men are wealthy, rich, living with much spectacle. Sometimes however they are involved in uncertainties and hostility. Especially if the star <Jupiter> is found to be setting, they resort to greater showiness and make a pretense of the truth.

[COMMENT] Jupiter and Sun have similar connotations - fame, power, distinction, wealth - and the two amplify each other here. There can also be a negative side where wealth becomes pretentiousness and pride becomes showiness, bragging. That is the two similar planets together out of balance, amplifying each other's faults.

Jupiter and the Moon are good, acquisitive: they cause men to be masters of adornments and slaves, and they bestow distinguished offices and ranks. They cause men to benefit from women and distinguished individuals, to be treated well by family and children, and to be thought worthy of gifts and honors. They make treasurers, men who lend much, who are trusted, and who find treasures and become wealthy.

[COMMENT] The Moon is adornments, slaves, women, family. Add in Jupiter and you are masters of all those. This is Jupiter's honor and power plus Moon's connection with family, women and groups of people.

Jupiter and Mars make glorious and showy characters, friends of the great or of kings, distinguished governors and receivers of stipends, those making a career in public affairs or in campaigns, and those considered worthy of honor and status, but uncertain in their livelihoods and habits, tossing away their possessions.

[COMMENT] Jupiter amplifies the best of Mars, gives honor and strength, and there is also some of the instability and carelessness of Mars here, a recklessness. Mars is not a planet that thinks ahead or uses foresight.

Jupiter and Venus are good, in harmony, productive of rank and profits, bringing new acquisitions, gifts, adornments, control over slaves, rulerships, the begetting of children, high priesthoods, preeminence among the masses, honors of garlands and gold crowns. These stars make men who are worthy of statues and images, but they also make them subject to ups and downs with respect to marriages and children.

[COMMENT] This is similar to the description for Jupiter and the Moon; Venus and the Moon do have a lot of common attributions. This combines Jupiter signifying rank, honor and profits, plus Venus signifying adornment, garlanding and decorating, statues and images. Marriage and children are also connected to Venus.

Jupiter and Mercury are good, in harmony, and supervisory. They make men who are managers, overseers of affairs, in posts of trust and administration. They make men who are successful as secretaries and accountants and who are respected in education. These are approachable people with many friends, judged worthy of pay and stipends. If Jupiter and Mercury are found in operative signs, they make men discoverers of treasures, or moneylenders who profit from cash deposits.

[COMMENT] This combines Jupiter's power and honor plus Mercury's skills in organizing, in education and in commerce. It is a natural positive combination.

Jupiter - Abu Mashar

6 As for Jupiter, his nature is heating, moist, airy, temperate.

7 And he indicates the soul which nourishes, life, animal bodies, children, the children of children, embryos, scholars, legal experts, making judgments between people, acting justly, verification, understanding, sages, the interpretation of dreams, sincerity, truth, religion, worship, modesty, piety, reverence, being god-fearing, unification, insight into religion, uprightness, endurance, and [such a man] will be praised, and have a good reputation.

8 And he indicates suffering, zeal, and sometimes recklessness and haste will befall him, and endangering himself after being unhurried and the endurance.

9 And he indicates prosperity, success, defeat for all who resist him, dignity, leadership, authority, kings, the nobles and the mighty, the greatness of [one's] good luck, comfort and delight, desire for assets and collecting them as well as exploiting them for profit, riches and the goodness of [one's] condition in luxury and wealth, and his spirit will be lucky in every matter, and [his] character good, [and it indicates] charitable giving, generosity, granting, being open-handed (as well as boasting [about it]), being unrestrained [in his] soul, sincerity of affection, a love of leadership over the people of cities, and a love of those having importance as well as great people, and an inclination towards them, and assisting the people in things.

10 And he indicates the love of building, and magnificent dwellings filled with people, insight into things, fidelity in [one's] commitments, fulfilling what one is entrusted with, being indulgent, fun, jokes, beauty, adornment, coquettishness, joy, laughter, an abundance of speech, eloquence of the tongue; everyone who meets with him will delight in him, and he indicates an abundance of sexual intercourse,

138

love of the good and hatred of evil, making peace between people, commanding what is beneficial and forbidding what is detestable.

[COMMENT]

Verse 7 covers an important theme for Jupiter, the relation to religion and piety, to law including religious and moral law, and to the kinds of virtues a person would have who valued those highly - sincerity, piety, truth. Related to that is wisdom, including that coming from above and within, hence interpretation of dreams.

There is also a legal side to these associations - being expert on law, being a fair judge. The religious and legal sides of Jupiter blend together, as they did in earlier cultures where you can't draw a hard line between religious and political law.

Verse 8 talks about zeal, recklessness, haste. This is somewhat atypical of Jupiter and more like Mars. Here could be related to an enthusiasm or ebullience of Jupiter getting carried away to an extreme.

In verse 9, as in Valens, Jupiter is linked to prosperity, success, also generosity and charitable giving. Jupiter shows ruler over cities who loves and cares for the city and the people in it, hence helpful to all. Jupiter is benevolence, magnanimity.

Verse 10 is the large side of Jupiter, loving magnificent large and beautiful buildings filled with crowds of people. A building like the Taj Mahal is very Jupiterian.

This verse also includes enjoyment in large and lavish ways, indulging in fun and pleasurable activities including an abundance of sex.

As we saw before, there is the moral side of Jupiter, siding with moral and religious law and righteousness, hence love of good and hatred of evil. Jupiter harmonizes and brings together, so being peacemaker is included.

Jupiter - Al-Biruni

NATURES OF THE PLANETS

Jupiter is moderately warm and moist. The greater benefic. Male. Diurnal. Sweet, bittersweet, delicious. Dust color and white mixed with yellow and brown, shining, glittering. Moderate, complete, pleasant, best and easiest things. Moderation, solidity, smoothness.

BUILDINGS

Royal palaces, mansions of the nobility, mosques, pulpits, Christian churches and synagogues, science, books, ordinary vessels, teacher's houses, vessels of leadworkers.

[COMMENT] The associations here tie together richness, largeness and nobility, the religious connotation, and a connection to teaching and science. Religious law, moral law, political law and scientific law are all interwoven concepts. There is some overlap here between Jupiter and Mercury.

RELATIONS AND CONNECTIONS, FIGURE AND FACE

Children and grandchildren. Fine figure, round face, thick prominent nose, large eyes, frank look, small beard, abundant curly hair reddish.

[COMMENT] Here I think the connection with children is not being a child, but having children, hence fruitfulness and ability to give life. Being an outer planet, Jupiter is associated with the later mature years of life, the years when one is typically at a peak of power, influence and affluence, prior to old age which belongs to Saturn. By the time of the mature years it is common to have a good number of children.

DISPOSITION AND MANNERS

Good disposition, inspiring, intelligent, patient, high-minded, devout, chaste, administering justice, truth-telling, learned, generous, noble, cautious in friendship, egoistic, friend of good government, eager for education, an honorable trusty and responsible custodian, religious.

[COMMENT] These are the internal or character traits that go with Jupiter's association with religion and law.

ACTIVITIES, INSTINCTS AND MORALS

Friendliness, a peacemaker, charitable, devoted to religion and good works, responsible, uxorious, laughing, eloquent, eager for wealth, in addition to affability some levity and recklessness.

[COMMENT] Along with the good moral qualities we again see the possibility of recklessness, getting carried away, not taking things seriously. This is Jupiter's expansiveness out of balance.

CLASSES OF PEOPLE

Kings, viziers, nobles, lawyers, magnates, merchants, the rich and their sycophants.

RELIGIONS, PICTURES OF PLANETS

Christians and those dressed in white. A young man with a drawn sword in the right hand and a bow and a rosary in the left, on horseback; another picture: man on a throne, clad in variously colored robes, a rosary in the left hand.

TRADES AND PROFESSIONS

Noble actions, good government, religion, doing good; interpretation of dreams; goldsmith's work, banking; selling old gold and silver, white clothes, grapes and sugarcane.

[COMMENT] We see an emphasis here on government, religion, wisdom. There is also the association with wealth and money including dealing with commerce and banking, so again we have an overlap with Mercury. The other items combine Jupiter's mercantile side with selling Jupiterian sorts of things that are beautiful, clean, pleasant, sweet, the kinds of goods associated with abundance. These are signs of the Good Life, which is a very Jupiterian concept.

Jupiter - William Ramesey

Jupiter when he is Lord of the year and well dignified, the King shall do Justice, and it shall be happy for those that are Noblemen, Judges, Councellors of the Law, and men of all sorts of religious orders shall be in a successful, happy, pleasant and good condition, and shall live pleasantly and contentedly, in honor, and also great esteem; and the people shall also be in a good and prosperous condition, and shall receive good from the King and Superiors, and they from the people, and the year shall be healthy, plentiful and good, a temperate air, rain, fair weather, and frost in due season, &c.

But if Jupiter be weak, judge the contrary, according to the strength of the affliction wherewith he is afflicted and impedited.

Of Humors, he is author of the Sanguine or best complexion, moist, temperate, sound, healthful &c.

Quality of men, in general this is to be understood, as indeed most of the qualities and attributions aforesaid: he signifies Judges, Councellors, all Ecclesiastical men both Priests and Levites, Chancellors, lawyers, or those that follow the law from the highest to the lowest, all Scholars and Students in general, Clothiers, Woollen-Drapers.

When he is weak, he signifies Mountebanks, Quack-salvers, Empericks, Cheaters, Takers of Bribes, &c.

He is author of sobriety and temperance.

Of men, he signifies, Religious men, Church men &c.

Of herbs, Nutmegs, Sugar, Mace, Cloves Strawberries, Balm, Wild Marjoram, Sweet Marjoram or Oregano, Wheat, Basil, Licorice, Pomegranates, and all such herbs as are helpful to obstructions of the liver, &c.

Of Birds, he ruleth the Eagle, Peacock, Pheasant, Partridge, Stork, Lark, Bees &c.

Of Stones, the Topaz, Amethyst, Marble, Emerald, Sapphire, Hyacinth, Free-stone &c.

Of Metals, Tin, Pewter &c.

Of Fish, the Whale, Serpent, Dolphin &c.

Of Beasts, the Sheep, Unicorn, Doe, Hart, Stag, Ox, Elephant, and all such beasts as are beneficial and useful to mankind.

Of Places, Churches, neat and curious places, Gardens, Synods, Courts of Justice, Wardrobes, Palaces, Sweet places, Oratories.

He commonly causeth pleasant healthful weather, serenity, Temperate air &c.

In Journeys, when he is Significator, he denotes pleasant travel, good success, safety, health and mirth.

Of Diseases, Infirmities of the Livers, Obstructions, Pleurisies, Apoplexies, inflammation of the lungs, infirmities of the left ear, palpitation of the heart, cramps, pain in the back, all infirmities of the reins [kidneys], or proceeding from corruption of blood and putrefactions therein, Squinzies, Fevers proceeding from abundance of blood; all griefs in the head, pulse, seed, arteries; convulsions, prickings and shootings in the body, &c.

Jupiter - William Lilly

Jupiter is placed next to Saturn (amongst the Ancients) you shall sometimes find him called Zeus, or Phaeton: He is the greatest in appearance to our eyes of all the Planets (the Sun, Moon and Venus excepted;)

[COLOR, MOTION.] In his Colour he is bright, clear, and of an Azure colour. In his Motion he exceeds Saturn, finishing his course through the twelve Signs in twelve years: his middle motion is 4 min. 59 seconds: his Diurnal motion is 8,10,12 or 14 mm. hardly any more.

[HOUSES.] He hath two of the twelve Signs of the Zodiac for his houses, viz. Sagittarius his Day-house, and Pisces his Night-house. He receives Detriment in Gemini and Virgo. He is Exalted in Cancer, hath his Fall in Capricorn.

[NATURE.] He is a Diurnal, Masculine Planet, Temperately Hot and Moist, Airy, Sanguine, the greater Fortune, author of Temperance, Modesty, Sobriety, Justice.

[MANNERS & ACTIONS WHEN WELL PLACED.) Then is he Magnanimous, Faithful, Bashful, Aspiring in an honourable way at high matters, in all his actions a Lover of fair Dealing, desiring to benefit all men, doing Glorious things, Honourable and Religious, of sweet and affable Conversation, wonderfully indulgent to his Wife and Children, reverencing Aged men, a great Reliever of the Poor, full of Charity and Godliness, Liberal, hating all Sordid actions, Just, Wise, Prudent, Thankful, Virtuous: so that when you find Jupiter the significator of any man in a Question, or Lord of his Ascendant in a Nativity, and well dignified, you may judge him qualified as above said.

[WHEN ILL.] When Jupiter is unfortunate, then he wastes his Patrimony, suffers every one to cozen him, is Hypocritically Religious, Tenacious, and stiff in maintaining false Tenets in Religion; he is

Ignorant, Careless, nothing Delightful in the love of his Friends; of a gross, dull Capacity, Schismatical, abating himself in all Companies, crouching and stooping where no necessity is.

[CORPORATURE] He signifies an upright, straight and tall Stature; brown, ruddy and lovely Complexion; of an oval or long Visage, and it full and fleshy; high Forehead; large gray Eyes; his Hair soft, and a kind of auburn brown; much Beard; a large, deep Belly: Strong proportioned Thighs and Legs; his feet long, being the most indecent parts of his whole Body; in his Speech he is Sober, and of grave Discourse.

[ORIENTAL.] The skin more dear, his complexion Honey-color, or betwixt a white and red, sanguine, ruddy Colour; great Eyes, the body more fleshy, usually some Mole or Scar in the right Foot.

[OCCIDENTAL.] A pure and lovely Complexion, the Stature more short, the Hair a light Brown, or near a dark Flaxen; smooth, bald about the Temple or Forehead.

[MEN & THEIR QUALITY IN GENERAL.] He signifies Judges, Senators, Counselors, Ecclesiastical men, Bishops, Priests, Ministers, Cardinals, Chancellors, Doctors of the Civil Law, young Scholars and Students in an University or College, Lawyers. Clothiers, Woollen-Drapers.

[DISEASES.] Pleurisies, all Infirmities in the Liver, left Ear, Apoplexies, Inflammation of the Lungs, Palpitations and Trembling of the Heart, Cramps, pain in the Backbone, all Diseases lying in the Veins or Ribs, and proceeding from corruption of Blood, Squinzies, Windiness, all Putrification in the Blood, or Fevers proceeding from too great abundance thereof.

[SAVORS.] He governeth the Sweet or well scented Odors; or that Dour which in smell is no way extreme or offensive.

[COLOURS.] Sea-green or Blue, Purple, Ash-color, a mixt Yellow and Green.

[HERBS & DRUGS.] Cloves and Clove-sugar, Mace, Nutmeg, Gilly-flower, the Straw-berry, the herb Balsam, Bettony, Centory, Flax, Arss-smart, Fumitory, Lung-wort, Pimpernel, Walwort, Orangy or Wild Margorane, Rhubarb, Self-heal, Borage, Buglosse, Wheat, Willow-herb, Thorough-Leaf, Violets, Laskwort, Liverwort, Bazil, Pomegranates, Pyony, Licorice, Mint, Mastix, the daisy, Feversend, Saffron.

[PLANTS & TREES.] Cherry-tree, Birch-tree, Mulberry-tree, Corall-tree, the Oak, Barburies, Olive, Gooseberries, Almond-tree, the Ivy, Manna, Mace, the Vine, the Fig-tree, the Ash, the Pear-tree, the Hazel, the Beech-tree, the Pine, Raisins.

[BEASTS.] The Sheep, the Heart or Stag, the Doe, the Ox, Elephant, Dragon, Tyger, Unicorn, those Beasts which are Mild and Gentle, and yet of great benefit to Mankind, are appropriate to him.

[BIRDS.] The Stork, the Snipe, the Lark, the Eagle, the Stock-dove, the Partridge, Bees, Pheasant, Peacock, the Hen.

(FISHES.] The Dolphin, the Whale, Serpent, Sheath-fish or River Whale.

[PLACES.] He delighteth in or near Altars of Churches, in public Conventions, Synods, Convocations, in Places neat, sweet, in Wardrobes, Courts of Justice, Oratory.

[MINERAL & PRECIOUS STONES.] Tin, Amethyst, the Sapphire, the Smarage or Emerald, Hyacinth, Topaz, Chrystal, Bezoar, Marble, and that which in England we call Free-stone.

[WEATHER.] He usually produceth serenity, pleasant and healthful North Winds, and by his gentle Beams all allays the ill weather of any former Malignant Planets.

[WINDS.] He governeth the North Wind, that part which tendeth to the East.

[ORB.] His Radiation or Orb, is nine degrees before and after any of his aspect.

[GENERATION.] He governeth the second and tenth month; his proper seat in man is the Liver; and in the Elements he ruleth the Air.

[AGE.] Men of middle age, or of a full Judgment and Discretion.

[CLIMATE.] He governeth the second Climate.

[ANGEL.] Zadkiel.

[DAY OF THE WEEK.] Thursday, and rules the first hour after Sun rise, and the eighth; the length of the Planetary hour you must know by the rising of the Sun, and a Table hereafter following.

All Planets except Mars are friends to Jupiter. In gathering any Herb appropriate to Jupiter, see that he be very powerful either in Essential or Accidental Dignities, and the Moon in some manner in good aspect with him, and if possible, let her be in some of his Dignities, &c.

Jupiter - General Notes

Modern astrology often sums up Jupiter by the one word, Expansion. That is part of the meaning, but by no means all. Expansion is part of a larger connected group of concepts.

Jupiter is the planet just below Saturn. Along with the Sun they are the largest planets, so each of them has an association with rulership, power, control. In the mythology as it was interpreted by Plato, Proclus and others in the Platonic tradition, Jupiter or Zeus is the Demiurge, the creator or architect god who formed the manifest universe along the lines of patterns revealed from higher levels through Saturn. Jupiter is also referred to as a fabricator, working with existing materials to shape and order them. In terms of the planetary mythology you can think of Saturn as giving creator and architect Jupiter the laws and patterns that Jupiter looks to as the template for his work.

This means that Jupiter is not just expansion but creation, giving order, bringing things together to make a harmonious whole. This is not creation out of nothing, but rather creation as giving shape, order, form and harmony. Given that context, Jupiter as expansion, creation and rulership all connect conceptually. Jupiter creates and sustains a benevolent order. Jupiter is associated with Kings, with creation, and with controlling, ruling and directing, and also with law.

Jupiter is often associated with religion, with philosophy and morality, and this is not separate from the other meanings. In the traditional world, creation, religion, law, morality and kingship are all intertwined. It is a single over-arching order with many dimensions. Religion points to an overall divine order that re-links us, connects us in a harmonious whole.

In more modern terms you could say Jupiter is related to spirituality, but that word has connotations today it did not have earlier. In the traditional world spirituality is not an issue of personal internal development, but rather it is more related to how a person is well integrated into the overall order of the universe. This goes with the general emphasis in traditional astrology on overall order rather than individual psychology. We will raise this point again when we talk about the traditional meanings of the Sun.

Being a benefic and concerned with harmonious order, Jupiter also has associations with grace and beauty, but not quite in the same way as the other benefic Venus. Venus is more about beauty, harmony and grace for its own sake, while with Jupiter has connotations of luxury, wealth, abundance which goes with his powers of creation and expansion. There is a largeness and sometimes an ostentatiousness to Jupiter that you do not have with Venus.

Saturn - Source Texts

The Planet Saturn - Prefatory Note

Most of the text in this section is taken from my previous book, *Saturn Through the Ages: Between Time and Eternity*. There are two exceptions. In the chapter from Abu Mashar I am using the more recent translation by Ben Dykes from the Arabic that is forthcoming this year (2020) in his translation of Abu Mashar's **Great Introduction**. The excerpt from William Ramesey is also new to this book.

In my book on Saturn I include the source texts I reference here and several more, including many excerpts from modern astrologers. I spend quite a bit of time in that book examining the change in meaning of Saturn from the traditional texts as we move into the modern era.

More importantly, I spend quite a bit of time talking about the difference in philosophy and worldview between traditional and modern astrology. I think that traditional astrology makes a lot more sense when you have an idea of the kind of context of philosophy that provided a supportive framework for understanding it. If the philosophy behind astrology is of interest to you, I encourage you to look into the Saturn book.

The comments in this section are more extensive than in the earlier sections of this book, especially the General Notes section. I find Saturn to be among the most interesting and complex of the planets, and it has a particular fascination for me. In that General Notes chapter for this section I am also casting a wider net, and spending time on the overall context of traditional astrology. That chapter touches on themes that apply to traditional astrology in ways that are wider than the specific planet Saturn.

Saturn - Valens

Saturn makes those born under him petty, malignant, care-worn, self-depreciating, solitary, deceitful, secretive in their trickery, strict, downcast, with a hypocritical air, squalid, black-clad, importunate, sad-looking, miserable, with a nautical bent, plying waterside trades. Saturn also causes humblings, sluggishness, unemployment, obstacles in business, interminable lawsuits, subversion of business, secrets, imprisonment, chains, griefs, accusations, tears, bereavement, capture, exposures of children.

Saturn makes serfs and farmers because of its rule over the land, and it causes men to be renters of property, tax farmers, and violent in action. It puts into one's hands great ranks and distinguished positions, supervisions, management of others' property, and the fathership of others' children.

Of materials, it rules lead, wood, and stone. Of the limbs of the body, it rules the legs, the knees, the tendons, the lymph, the phlegm, the bladder, the kidneys, and the internal, hidden organs. Saturn is indicative of injuries arising from cold and moisture, such as dropsy, neuralgia, gout, cough, dysentery, hernia, spasms. It is indicative of these syndromes: possession, homosexuality, and depravity. Saturn makes bachelors and widows, bereavements, and childlessness. It causes violent deaths by water, strangulation, imprisonment, or dysentery. It also causes falling on the face. It is the star of Nemesis; it is of the day sect. It is like castor in color and astringent in taste.

[COMMENT]

Note that there is a connection of Saturn with water in the earliest texts. In later texts this tends to be less emphasized or to disappear. We also see associations with traits that make a person small, or negative, or limited, or untrustworthy. Self-depreciating here means limiting or cutting down oneself. Also note the connection with the color black, and with bad fortune. Another cluster of meanings relates to deceiving, hiding, tricking or being hypocritical. If you think of being in the light as honest, then being in the darkness of Saturn is deceiving, hiding, dishonest.

This section includes problems, bad fortunes, death and events that block or limit. There are connections with things that take a long time or stretch on, and connections with secrecy, things that are hidden or in the dark.

We see the connection of Saturn with land, with what is hard and physical. This includes people who work with the land, as renters, as servants or as owner.

With the description of injuries and diseases we see the early connection of Saturn with cold and wet. In later quotes we will see Saturn associated with diseases related to the body drying up or becoming inflexible, like arthritis. The cold and dry associations with become more dominant as we move through time. The cold/dry association relates to the system of humors where Saturn is classified as melancholic, the most cold and dry of the planets. Where planets are associated with a system of classification, the meanings that don't fit within the classification tend to fall away.

These are associations of Saturn with things evil, or corrupt, sinful or deviant.

This connects Saturn with losses by death, or from an inability to give birth.

All of these Saturn associations are bad fortune related to death, and again the association with water.

Nemesis is the Greek goddess of vengeance or retributive justice, a punishment that is deserved, though one that could be delayed. This highlights a connection of Saturn with justice, judgment, the punitive side of the law. Earlier we saw an association of Saturn with law as related to authority.

Astringent tastes make the mouth shrivel or shrink or dry up, so it is related to Saturn being cold and dry.

Saturn and the other Planets

[TEXT] When **Saturn and Jupiter** are together, they are in agreement with each other, and they bring about benefits from legacies and adoptions, and they cause men to be masters of property consisting of land, to be guardians, managers of others' property, stewards, and tax gatherers.

[COMMENT] These meanings are almost all positive, and combine authority and control. Legacies are inheritances that come from deaths. We also have the connection again of Saturn with land, so controlling the wealth of land.

[TEXT] **Saturn and Mars** are hostile, productive of reversals and ruin. They bring family quarrels, disharmony, and hatred, along with treachery, plots, malevolence, and trials. However, if these stars are not in their own or in operative signs, and if they have benefics in aspect, they produce distinguished and noble nativities, although unsteady in their happiness and prone to unexpected dangers and treachery.

[COMMENT] The two malefics together are violent and destructive. The references to nobility refers to the power that these malefics could exert if in a prominent position. Whether powerful or not there is an instability and lack of trustworthiness to the action of these two planets combined. You would not want to be on the bad side of a person with these traits.

[TEXT] **Saturn and Mercury** are allies and productive of activities/employment. They do, however, bring slanders about religion, lawsuits, and debts, as well as disturbances about written matters and money. On the other hand, these stars make men who are not without resources and not unintelligent, with much experience and awareness, and who are curious, far-seeing scholars, seekers after mystic lore, revering the gods, but with much on their consciences.

[COMMENT] Combining Saturn with Mercury's rulership of commerce and we get control of money. Mercury is also associated with learning, which combines with Saturn to give depth, profundity, a mystic side, a researcher into hidden truths. Overall Saturn and Mercury together is seen as a positive combination.

[TEXT] **Saturn and Venus** act harmoniously with respect to activities/employment: they promote success with respect to entanglements and marriage, agreeing and beneficial only for a time, not to the end. Indeed they cause abuse, divorces, inconstancy, and death, often entangling men with the base-born and the lowly, and causing them to fall into harm and lawsuits.

[COMMENT] Most of these relate to Venus as associated with relationships and marriage. The Saturn Venus connection is good when it is stable, but filled with problems and strife when debilitated. You also have the connection of Saturn with death.

[TEXT] **Saturn and the Moon** are beneficial, productive of money, estates, ship ownership, and profits from the deceased, especially if the Moon happens to be in the part of its orbit just following first visibility and has benefics in aspect. Then it causes association with the great, gifts, and the discomfiture of enemies. This combination, however, is unsteady with respect to possession, and with respect to women it is insecure and painful because of separations, hatred, and grief. It also produces bodily suffering, sudden fits, pains of the governing faculties and nerves, as well as the deaths of important figures. ·

[COMMENT] This is the Moon ruling changing fortunes, and again we see the connection of Saturn with death, the deceased, and legacies. The Moon is also related to women and thus to separations. The Moon relates to bodily health, which combined with Saturn gives physical suffering.

[TEXT] **Saturn and the Sun** are at odds, giving and taking away possessions and friendships maliciously. Therefore those born under such a juncture suffer secret enmities and threats from great persons and are plotted against by some and live hated to the end. Playing their part well, they outlive most of their enemies. They are, however, not without resources, but are disturbed and long-suffering. They are self-controlled in this onslaught of reversals.

[COMMENT] Most of these Saturn-Sun meanings come from the fact that the two planets are in opposition in the Zodiac signs they rule, Saturn in Aquarius opposite Sun in Leo. We have the hottest and brightest planet opposite the coldest and darkest. Saturn stands for the opposition aspect in general, and thus anything that blocks or hinders.

Saturn - Abu Ma'Shar

3 As for Saturn, his nature is cooling, drying, black bile, dark, harsh in coarseness; but sometimes it is cooling [and] moist, heavy, stinking air.

4 And he is of much eating, sincere in [his] affection, and indicates works of moisture, plowing, farming, the masters of villages, the cultivation of lands, building, waters and rivers, the appraising of things, the apportioning of lands, wealth and an abundance of assets, those working with their hands, and avarice, harsh poverty, lowly people, travel on the seas, a long absence from the homeland, and distant, bad journeys, and delusion, malice, resentment, cunning, stratagems, deception, treachery, harm, anguish, solitude and little company with people, putting on airs, lack of restraint, haughtiness, conceit, boasting, those who enslave the people, managers for the Sultan, and every work [done] with evil, coercion, injustice, and anger; and fighters, chains, confinement, stocks, and imposing restrictions; and sincerity of speech, deliberateness, being unhurried, understanding, tested actions, examination, stubbornness, much thought, profundity, insistence, sticking to a single path, hardly ever getting angry (but if he did get angry he would not [be able to] control himself), not loving the good for anyone.

5 And he indicates old men, and the weighty (among people), fear, hardships, anxieties, sorrows, dejection, confusion, complications, difficulty, adversity, restriction, the ancestors, the dead, inheritances, lamentation, orphanhood, old things, grandfathers, fathers, older brothers, slaves, stable workers, misers, people who have a bad reputation, disgraced people, robbers, gravediggers, murdaqshes, body-snatchers, tanners, people who make things faulty, sorcerers, masters of social unrest, the riffraff, eunuchs, long thought but little speech, the knowledge of secrets (and no one knows what is in his soul, nor does he disclose it to [anyone]), being acquainted with every

abstruse matter, and it indicates leading an ascetic life and the devout people of religious communities.

[COMMENT]

Here we have the primary association of Saturn with dark and cold. Sometimes Saturn is cold and dry, sometimes cold and moist. Saturn is stinking as in something unpleasant or poisonous or rotting. Things which are rotting or decay are in the process of dying, and Saturn is associated with death.

We also see an association with true esteem, an earned or deserved respect.

Saturn relates to earth, and people who work the earth, and earth near water, so again we see the connection with moisture. The connection with measuring associates with limiting, dividing, delimiting or setting boundaries or frameworks.

Saturn also is connected to extremes related to wealth - affluence from controlling much, or poverty from being lowly, cast down. There is an association with greed as a moral corruption, and greed as wanting to clutch and control more than one's fair share.

We also see more connections with Saturn as clever, wise, crafty, action that is not overt and blunt but covert, in the darkness, hidden.

There are positive traits that can come with age here, qualities like perseverance and experience. We also have the wisdom that comes with age. This is Saturn as profundity, as deep rather than shallow. Saturn is deep in multiple senses of the term. We also have Saturn as hidden, taciturn, withdrawn, quiet, secretive. Saturnian religious traits are severe, self-limiting, and monastic. Saturn when reliable is truth and wisdom, Saturn when unreliable is falsehood, craftiness and deception.

Saturn - Al-Biruni

[NATURES OF THE PLANETS AND THEIR INDICATORS] Saturn is extremely cold and dry. The greater malefic. Male. Diurnal. Disagreeable and astringent, offensively acid, stinking, jet-black also black mixed with yellow, lead colour, pitch-dark.

Saturn: Coldest, hardest, most stinking and most powerful of things. Shortness, dryness, hardness, heaviness. Barren mountains.

[COMMENT] These associations are mainly from the cold dry humors, and associations with darkness and rotting.

[BUILDINGS AND COUNTRIES] Saturn: Underground canals and vaults, wells, old buildings, desolate roads, lairs of wild beasts, deserts full of them, stables for horses, asses, and camels, and elephant's houses.

[COMMENT] Saturn goes with dark places, isolated places, lowly animals or animals that are beasts carrying heavy burdens.

[RELATIONS AND CONNECTIONS, FIGURE, AND FACE] Saturn: Fathers, grandfathers, older brothers and slaves. Ugly, tall, wizened, sour face, large head, eyebrows joined, small eyes, wide mouth, thick lips, downcast look, much black hair, short neck, coarse hand, short fingers, awkward figure, legs crooked, big feet.

[DISPOSITION AND MANNERS] Saturn: Fearful, timid, anxious, suspicious, miserly, a malevolent plotter, sullen and proud, melancholy, truth-telling, grave, trusty, unwilling to believe good of anyone, engrossed in his own affairs and consequently indicates discord, and either ignorance or intelligence, but the ignorance is concealed.

[COMMENT] Saturn here is isolated, and again we see the association with things hidden, indirect, in the darkness, not open and honest, hence also suspicious, selfish.

[ACTIVITIES, INSTINCTS AND MORALS] Saturn: Exile and poverty, or wealth acquired by his own trickery and that of others, failure in business, vehemence, confusion, seeking solitariness, enslaving people by violence or treachery, fraud, weeping and wailing and lamentation.

[COMMENT] The ways listed here that Saturn gains wealth and control are negative - deception, violence, treachery.

[RELIGIONS, PICTURES OF PLANETS] Saturn: Jews and those who dress in black. Old man seated on a wolf, in his right hand the head of a man and in the left a man's hand; or according to another picture, mounted on a bright bay horse, on his head a helmet, in the left hand a shield and in the right a sword.

[COMMENT] Planets were associated with religions, and Saturn was associated with the Jews as the people of the Torah, the Law, just as Saturn is associated with law in general. This also relates to Judaism as being a very old religion, a fore-runner or ancestor of Christianity, which was associated with Jupiter, the next planet down. Saturn is the planet of Law as Jupiter is the planet of Mercy.

[TRADES, PROFESSIONS] Saturn: Building, paymaster, farming, reclaiming land and distribution of water, apportioning money and heritages, grave-digging; selling things made of iron, lead, bone, hair, copper, black slaves; knowledge used for bad purposes, such acts of government as lead to evil oppression, wrath, captivity, torture.

[COMMENT] Here are associations with land, or again land and water together, with death, and with lowly people. Again we see the connection with corrupt motives; Saturn is a corrupt or oppressive or evil ruler who causes pain and malice.

Saturn - William Ramesey

[TEXT] Saturn well fortified, and Lord of the year in any annual revolution, signifies that the people shall that year, or during that revolution, build and erect houses; shall make many alterations in Fabrics, and shall abound in all things: the earth shall be fruitful, and the people shall be in esteem and honor with all their neighbors; the husbandman shall exceedingly increase his store and wealth, and be successful in his labors

[NOTE] Fabrics is used in a wider sense here, not just as cloth, but as things which are fabricated or constructed, hence different kinds of physical structures that last.

[TEXT] But if Saturn be Lord of the year and weak, there shall be much cold during that Revolution, great and grievous infirmities, and men shall sustain much sorrow, losses and crosses, and great damage by storms, wind and rain... and old men and women shall die.

Of Humors, he is author of Melancholy. And such men if they take to love any one, let them be man or woman (which happeneth but very seldom) they love most constantly and entirely; and if they hate (as most commonly they do) they hate to the death, and with a perpetual hatred, hardly to be removed.

If he be fortunate, of professions and Mastery, he denotes such as are profound and occult, antiquities, things and callings belonging to labor, care and rarities, and such as belong or have any relation to water, or near water; Sailors, Tankard-Bearers, Plumbers, Ship-Carpenters, and the like; and such as belong to the earth, as Curriers, Broom-men, Bearers of dead corpses Hostlers, Brick-makers, Plow-men, Scavengers, Colliers, Ditchers, Carters, Chandlers, Gardeners, Herds-men, Dyers of black cloth, Shepherds, Coach-men and Cowherds, Brick-layers, &c.

When unfortunate, he denotes generally laborers, employers of Jakes, Diggers of Coal-pits, and the like sordid and base occupations.

Quality of men in general, he signifieth fathers, grand-fathers, old men, day-laborers, Beggars, Clowns, Husbandmen, Monks, Jesuits &c.

[NOTE] Clowns means idiots, someone mentally deficient, and not a comic actor.

[TEXT] Herbs: Hemlock, Starwort, Bears-foot, Wolf-bane, Fern, Henbane, Burdock, Parsnip, Mandrake, Vervine, Nightshade Moss, Spinach, Cumin, Hemp, Yew-Tree.

Birds: Crow, Owl, Crane, Thrush, Ostrich, Lapwing, Peacock, Bat, Blackbird, Cuckoo.

Stones subject to him are the Sapphire, Lapis Lazuli, or that stone of which Azure is made, unpolished black and bluish stones.

Minerals, he governeth Lead, the Load-stone, the dross of all Metals.

Fishes, the Tortoise eel, and shell-fish.

Beasts, the Ass, Cat, Hare, Mouse, Mole, Dog, Wolf, Bear, Elephant, Basilisk, Crocodile, Scorpion, Serpent, Adder, Toad, Hog, all manner of creeping creatures breeding in putrefaction.

Places, he delighteth in deserts, woods, obscure valleys, dens, caves, holes, sepulchres, Church-yards, ruinous buildings, coal-pits, sinks, muddy dirty stinking places, wells, and houses of offices.

[NOTE] Sinks refers to holes in the earth with water, and not just our household fixture.

[TEXT] Weather, cloudy, dark, obscure air, cold and hurtful, thick, black and condense clouds.

In long journeys when he is Significator, he portends long and laborious travel, perilous dangers and imprisonments.

Diseases cause by Saturn, are the Falling-sickness, Phlegmatic humors, Defluctions, Melancholy, Leprosy, Fistulas, Aches and Colds in the Joints, Deafness, Tooth-ache, pains in the bones, in the bladder, all cold diseases, the Gout, Scab, Palsy, Consumptions, Quartan Agues, Chin-Cough, Cattarhs &c.

Saturn - William Lilly

[NAMES] He is called usually Saturn, but in some Authors Chronor Phoenon, Falcifer.

[COLOUR] He is the supremest or highest of all Planets; is placed betwixt Jupiter and the Firmament, he is not very bright or glorious, nor doth he twinkle or sparkle, but is of a Pale, Wan or Leaden, Ashy colour slow in motion.

[MOTION] Finishing his Course through the twelve signs of the Zodiac in 29 years, 157 days, or thereabouts; his middle motion is two minutes and one second; his diurnal motion sometimes is three, four, five, or six minutes, or seldom more.

[LATITUDE] His greatest North Latitude from the Ecliptic is two degrees 48 minutes; his South Latitude from the Ecliptic is two degrees 49 minutes; and more then this he hath not.

[HOUSES] In the Zodiac he hath two of the twelve Signs for his Houses, viz. Capricorn his Night-house, Aquarius his Day-house; he has his Exaltation in Libra, he receives his Fall in Aries; he rejoiceth in the sign Aquarius.

He continueth Retrograde 140 dayes. He is five days in his first station before Retrogradation, and so many in his second station before Direction.

[NATURE] He is a Diurnal Planet, Cold and Dry (being far removed from the heat of the Sun) and moist Vapours, Melancholic, Earthly, Masculine, the greater Infortune, author of Solitariness, Malevolent, &c.

[MANNERS & ACTIONS, WHEN WELL DIGNIFIED] Then he is profound in Imagination, in his Acts severe, in words reserved, in speaking and giving very spare, in labour patient, in arguing or disputing grave, in obtaining the goods of this life studious and solicitous, in all manner of actions austere.

[WHEN ILL DIGNIFIED] Then he is envious, covetous, jealous and mistrustful, timorous, sordid, outwardly dissembling, sluggish, suspicious, stubborn, a contemner of women, a close liar, malicious, murmuring, never contented, ever repining.

[CORPORATURE] Most part his Body more cold and dry, of a middle stature; his complexion pale, swartish or muddy, his Eyes little and black, looking downward, a broad Forehead, black or sad Hair, and it hard or rugged, great Ears; hanging, lowring Eye-brows, thick Lips and Nose, a rare or thin Beard, a lumpish, unpleasant Countenance, either holding his Head forward or stooping, his Shoulders broad and large, and many times crooked, his Belly somewhat short and lank, his Thighs spare; lean and not long; his Knees and Feet indecent, many times shoveling or hitting one against another, &c.

[SATURN ORIENTAL] You must observe, if Saturn be Oriental of the Sun, the stature is more short, but decent and well composed.

[OCCIDENTAL] The man is more black and lean, and fewer Hairs; and again, if he want latitude, the body is more lean, if he have great latitude, the body is more fat or fleshy; if the latitude be Meridionall or South, more fleshy, but quick in motion. If the latitude be North, hairy and much flesh.

Saturn in his first station, a little fat. In his second station, fat, ill favoured Bodies, and weak; and this observe constantly in all the other Planets.

[QUALITY OF MEN.] In general he signifieth Husbandmen, Clowns, Beggars, Day-labourers, Old-men, Fathers, Grand-fathers, Monks, Jesuits, Sectarists.

[PROFESSION.] Curriers, Night-farmers, Miners under ground, Tinners, Potters, Broom-men, Plumbers, Brick-makers, Malsters,

Chimney-sweepers, Sextons of Churches, Bearers of dead corpses, Scavengers, Hostlers, Colliers, Carters, Gardiners, Ditchers, Chandlers, Dyers of Black cloth, an Herdsman, Shepherd or Cow-keeper.

[SICKNESSES.] All Impediments in the right Ears, Teeth, all quartan Agues proceeding of cold, dry and melancholy Distempers, Leprosies, Rheumes, Consumptions, black Jaundices, Palsies, Tremblings, vain Fears, Fantasies, Dropsy, the Hand and Footgout, Apoplexies, Dog-hunger, too much flux of the Hemorroids, Ruptures if in Scorpio or Leo, in any ill aspect with Venus.

[SAVORS.] Sour, Bitter, Sharp, in mans body he principally ruleth the Spleen.

[HERBS.] He governeth Beirsfoot, Starwort, Woolf-bane, Hemlock, Ferne, Hellebore the white and black, Henbane, Ceterach or Fingerferne, Clotbur or Burdock, Parsnip, Dragon, Pulse, Vervine, Mandrake, Poppy, Mosse, Nightshade, Bythwind, Angelica, Sage, Box, Tutfan, Orage or golden Hearb, Spinach, Shepherds Purse, Cumin, Horitaile, Fumitory.

[PLANTS and TREES.] Tamarisk, Savine, Sene, Capers, Rue or Hearbgrice, Polipody, Willow or Sallow Tree, Yew-tree, Cypress tree, Hemp, Pine-tree.

[BEASTS, &c.] The Ass, Cat Hare, Mouse, Mole, Elephant, Bear, Dog, Wolf, Basilisk, Crocodile, Scorpion, Toad, Serpent, Adder, Hog, all manner of creeping Creatures breeding of putrification, either in the Earth, Water or Ruins of Houses.

[FISHES, BIRDS, &c.] The Eel, Tortoise, Shell-fishes. The Bat or Blood-black, Crow, Lapwing, Owle, Gnat, Crane, Peacock, Grashopper, Thrush, Blackbird, Ostrich, Cuckoo.

[PLACES.] He delights in Deserts, Woods, obscure Vallies, Caves, Dens, Holes, Mountains, or where men have been buried, Church-yards, &c. Ruinous Buildings, Cole-mines, Sinks, Dirty or Stinking Muddy Places, Wells and Houses of Offices, &c.

[MINERALS.] He ruleth over Lead, the Lead-stone, the Dross of all Metals, as also, the Dust and Rubbish of every thing.

[STONES.) Sapphire, Lapis Lazuli, all black, ugly Country Stones not polishable, and of a sad ashy or black colour.

[WEATHER.] He causeth Cloudy, Dark, obscure Air, cold and hurtful, thick, black and cadense Clouds: but of this more particularly in a Treatise by itself.

[WINDS.] He delighteth in the East quarter of Heaven, and causeth Eastern Winds, at the time of gathering any Planet belonging to him, the Ancients did observe to turn their faces towards the East in his hour, and he, if possible, in an Angle, either in the Ascendant, or tenth, or eleventh house, the Moon applying by a Trine or Sextile to him.

[ORB.] His Orb is nine degrees before and after; that is, his influence begins to work, when either he applies, or any Planet applies to him, and is within nine degrees of his aspect, and from that aspect.

[YEARS.] In Generation he ruleth the first and eighth month after Conception.

As to Age, he relates to decrepit old men; Fathers, Grandfathers, the like in Plants, Trees, and all living Creatures.

[ANGEL.] Its Cassiel, alias Captiel.

His friends are Jupiter, Sun and Mercury, his enemies Mars and Venus. We call Saturday his day, for then he begins to rule at Sun rise, and ruleth the first hour and eighth of that day.

Saturn - General Notes

I have a hunch that Saturn as cold and damp is an earlier attribution than cold and dry. In the system of the 4 humors Saturn is categorized as melancholic, cold and dry. This superseded the earlier association with water and damp, although we do see the association of Saturn with water throughout the tradition.

A lot of the meanings of Saturn come from its opposition to the lights, primarily the Sun, but also the Moon. The cluster of meanings for Saturn come from its position in the Thema Mundi and the primary aspect of opposition in that diagram. There is a geometrical underpinning to the meanings of the planet. If we take a table of opposites and put the Sun in one column across from Saturn, we see several of the most important dimensions of Saturn's meaning.

Sun	Saturn
hot and dry	cold and damp
light	dark
day	night
summer	winter
revealed	concealed
high	low
height	depth

Both Sun and Moon are related to physical vitality, and Saturn is opposite both. Some meanings are from the opposition aspect itself - whatever blocks, delays, opposes.

168

Saturn's Place in the Traditional Cosmos

There are several other core principles that are derived from the physical characteristics of the planet and its location in the traditional cosmos. Some of the meanings come from Saturn being the planet furthest from the heat of the Sun, thus the extreme of cold and of dark. Saturn being the coldest, darkest and most distant planet is related to the opposition aspect and its place opposite the lights in Thema Mundi.

Saturn is a border planet at the edge of time and eternity, the unmoving and the moving. You have Saturn as borders, walls, structures, edges, containers, skin. Saturn on the edge of eternity also is the mediator of the eternal law and order of the heavens down into the mutable world. This is Saturn as judgment, related to the modern notion of karma, but also Saturn as wisdom meaning knowledge and understanding of those laws - combine law plus age and you get the wisdom of age. Saturn as the outermost planet is very much the planet of entire cycles, and the wisdom that comes from knowledge of the entire cycles.

As border or gateway between moving and unmoving, time and eternity, Saturn is death - and, as Bonatti pointed out, Saturn marks both the entry into time and the exit from time. This relates Saturn to the after death reckoning, the judgment where our lives are measured over against the eternal law. Saturn also comes to represent Time itself, the overall process, and thus also overall cycles, and the consequences of the passage of time.

Combine age plus cold plus damp and you get associations with decaying, rotting, unhealthy, diseased, dying. Some of the other meanings come from Saturn being the slowest moving planet, hence associated with things that take a long time, move slowly, or are associated with age.

We can derive some main clusters of attributions of Saturn from various combinations of the basic meanings we have listed here.

Time - Many of the meanings come from Saturn's being on the border of eternity and time. Hence Saturn is associated with the passage of time. This has other related themes.

- Old age, which is the effect of time, and an age where you are very aware of time. In turn, Saturn is also associated with the elders, the aged, and with previous generations.

- The wisdom of old age, when you have the perspective on cycles that comes from time passage.

- Decaying, falling apart, as part of the passage of time; thus also corruption, decay, disease. Saturn seems to be especially related to diseases that are cold, or dry things up, or diseases that are like rotting or decay, so a skin disease like leprosy would be Saturnian.

- Saturn is thus also related to death, the inevitable consequence of life in time.

- Saturn is tradition, that which is passed down in time.

- Saturn relates to suffering, the effect of time, decay, delay etc. on people.

- Saturn and suffering can relate to moral law, and then you get suffering well, or enduring suffering for others.

Borders and Structures - This meaning also comes from being a border planet between time and timeless. Saturn is associated with containers like bodies, the skin of the body, the structure, the bones and teeth.

- Borders delineate and separate us, so Saturn is aloneness, isolation, being confined in a border or structure. Part of life in time includes fragmentation into separate entities. We are no longer simply part of oneness, we are separate beings.

- Saturn relates to habit, which is a structure that is built from repeated action over time, an action like a groove that has its own momentum.

- In Aristotle the virtues are described as habits we need to build by repeated actions, so Saturn can also be discipline, creating good habits. Saturn can also be the inertia of long standing bad habits, and their consequences.

Cold and Damp - This is an early attribution that is likely related to being opposite the Sun, and to Saturn being connected with Winter. This includes rotting, decaying, which combines cold and damp with time. Saturn is linked to Winter, and old age and dying are the winter of a human life.

Law and Judgment - This is a rich association, related to Saturn as structure, and to Saturn as at the border of time and eternal. Hence Saturn mirrors the eternal laws and structures into time.

- This relates to judgment, the consequences of action.

- Moral and religious wisdom relate to knowledge and understanding of the laws. Thus we also get the connection with profundity and depth of thought.

- Saturn ties to duty, which is the obligation to learn and follow the moral laws.

- Law plus age gives tradition passed down. Thus, for instance, Saturn strong in the ninth house can indicate interest in traditional philosophy and astrology.

- Saturn relates to the virtues of humility and selfless service. If the Sun is affirmation of the self, then Saturn is the negation. If

Sun is egotism then Saturn is humility. Combine with duty to law and you get selfless service.

- Relate this to feelings of guilt, shame, fear, related to a moral law and the knowledge one has broken it.

- Consequences and judgment connect the concepts of law with time.

- In a larger sense Saturn is fate, fortune, providence, those things that happen to you because of the laws playing out over time.

- Saturn gives perspective, objectivity, which combines time with law with thought.

- With time you get a sense of history, of passage of time.

Opposition - Many of the meanings of Saturn are related to this basic aspect from the Thema Mundi where Saturn is in opposition to the Sun. Hence, we get Saturn as adversary, opposer, that which blocks and hinders. Delay is opposition over time.

Here are other meanings of Saturn, with some thoughts as to how they were derived from the core meanings we looked at.

Lowly, Poor, Despised - Saturn as low as opposed to Sun as high. This also can mean physically low, hence places underground like caves, or basements in buildings. This combines being low with being dark and hidden, and possibly cold and damp.

Deceitful, Cynical - Think of Saturn opposite Sun, which is wide open, visible and honest. Saturn in turn can be hidden, deliberately hiding or deceiving.

Evil, Malefic, Harmful - This is related to Saturn opposite the lights, and Saturn as opposition, so we have evil as opposition to good, separated off or in rebellion from the good. Malefic and moral evil aren't quite the same thing, and we will look at those concepts in more detail in a later essay.

All of these clusters of meaning of Saturn relate to just a few main starting points - Saturn as opposite the Sun and furthest from the Sun, and Saturn as the outermost planet on the border of time and eternity. These seem to be the main keys to Saturn's meaning.

Conclusion - Going Further

To conclude this book I would like to suggest some good ways to follow up on the material we have covered here.

Source Texts

The first and most obvious place to go is to the full source texts which are excerpted in this book. I recommend all of them, and there is full information on them in the bibliography. If you do nothing else, I very strongly urge you to get hold of a copy of William Lilly's **Christian Astrology**. I particularly like the two volume edition edited by the late David Roell and published by Astrology Classics. You will live with and learn from that book for all of the rest of your astrology career.

Traditional Source Texts

There are many, many other source texts worth reading, and I would like to mention a few of them here. The texts I mention here all have extensive sections on the planets. Information on these books is in the bibliography.

Firmicus Maternus, **Mathesis** - This book was originally in Latin and is from the fourth century. It has some lengthy sections on the planets meaning in the houses.

Abu Ma'shar, **On the Revolutions of the Years of Nativities** - This is an amazing and detailed book that lays out an entire suite of techniques that form a full predictive system. There are numerous sections that lay out the meanings of the planet in different predictive contexts.

Avraham Ben Meir Ibn Ezra, - **The Beginning of Wisdom**. Ibn Ezra (1089?-1164) was a well-known and widely learned Jewish scholar who made contributions to Hebrew grammar, biblical exegesis, philosophy, philology, poetry and mathematics. He also wrote an excellent series of textbooks on astrology which were influential in the Middle Ages. Ibn Ezra was strongly influence by the Arabic tradition. Three of his books were translated into English by Meira Epstein as part of Project Hindsight.

Reading Modern Astrologers

Once you get a grasp of the traditional meanings we have covered in this book, it is worth going back over modern astrology texts, paying attention to how they differ from traditional texts in numerous ways - the meanings of the planets, the way they are taught, and also the kinds of assumptions that modern astrologers have. Modern astrology lives in an entirely different world from much of traditional astrology, and it is worth becoming aware of that to understand why they come up with the meanings they use. I go into that in quite a bit of detail in my book on Saturn, where I examine several modern astrologers.

Learning Traditional Astrology

Finally, I would like to suggest some other books that I have written that are designed to be practical and user-friendly ways to approach working with traditional astrology.

My *Introduction to Traditional Natal Astrology* is a good place to start and stands by itself. I cover a lot of the basic building blocks of traditional astrology that are the core of the system. Much of the section of the current book on the context for understanding the planets is taken from my Introduction.

My book on *Using Dignities in Astrology* is a thorough and workable way to start using the system of of dignities and debilities used to weigh up the condition of the planets. This is right at the heart of traditional technique.

Conclusion - Going Further

For traditional predictive astrology, my book on ***The Cycle of the Year*** covers the core framework of the predictive system in Abu Ma'shar's book *On the Revolutions* which I mentioned earlier. I think my *Cycle* book makes a good introduction to Abu Ma'shar's text.

And finally, if you are interested in the philosophy and worldview of traditional astrology and how it differs from our modern world, my recent book, **Saturn Through the Ages: Between Time and Eternity**, goes into that in some depth. Most of the section on Saturn in the current book is taken from that book on Saturn. In that book I make the case that the traditional meanings of Saturn make most sense when you are familiar with the worldview in place in the traditional world, and I talk about how much of this worldview can still apply in our modern world. Philosophy is a pet interest of mine - I think of myself as a student of philosophy masquerading as an astrologer - and of the books I have written, this one is closest to my heart.

For advanced students and the Truly Ambitious, Ben Dykes plans to release his course in Traditional Astrology in the second half of 2020. See his site, https://BenDykes.com for details.

However you choose to proceed in your working with astrology, I hope that you have found this book to be a good source for deepening your understanding of the classical seven planets. They are, and always will be, at the very heart of astrology.

Bibliography

Abu Ma'shar, *The Great Introduction*, translated by Dykes, Benjamin N. PhD. D. Minneapolis, Cazimi Press, Forthcoming 2020.

_____ , *On the Revolutions of the Years of Nativities*, translated by Dykes, Benjamin N. PhD. D. Minneapolis, Cazimi Press, 2019.

Al-Biruni, *The Book of Instructions in the Elements of the Art of Astrology*. Bel Air MD, Astrology Classics, 2006.

Firmicus Maternus, Julius, *Mathesis*. Translated by James H. Holden. Tempe, AFA, 2011.

Holden, James Herschel, M.A., *Biographical Dictionary of Western Astrologers*. Tempe AZ, AFA, 2012.

Ibn-Ezra, Avraham, *The Beginning of Wisdom*. Translated by Meira Epstein. ARHAT, 1998.

Lilly, William, *Christian Astrology*. Edited by David Roell, Bel Air MD, Astrology Classics, 2004.

Obert, Charles, *Introduction to Traditional Natal Astrology*. Minneapolis, Almuten Press, 2015.

_____, *Using Dignities in Astrology*. Minneapolis, Almuten Press, 2018.

_____, *The Cycle of the Year: Traditional Predictive Astrology*. Minneapolis, Almuten Press, 2018.

_____, *The Lots of Fortune and Spirit: An Exploratory Study*. Minneapolis, Almuten Press, 2019.

Bibliography

_____, *Saturn Through the Ages: Between Time and Eternity*. Minneapolis, Almuten Press, 2019.

(Note that all of my books listed above are available in pdf download form at my website, https://studentofastrology.com.)

Ramesey, William, *Astrologia Restaurata, Or, Astrologie Restored Being an Introduction to the General and Chief Part of the Language of the Stars in Four Books*. Public Domain, 1653.

_____, *Astrology Restored*, modernized edition with annotations by Kim Farnell. Lulu.com, 2014.

Valens, Vettius, *Anthology*. Translated by Mark Riley. Available online at:
http://www.csus.edu/indiv/r/rileymt/Vettius%20Valens%20entire.pdf.

Lightning Source UK Ltd.
Milton Keynes UK
UKHW010636270521
384471UK00001B/61